The New China

The New China

Winifred Nelson Beechy

Foreword by J. Harry Haines

HERALD PRESS
Scottdale, Pennsylvania
Kitchener, Ontario
1982

Library of Congress Cataloging in Publication Data

Beechy, Winifred.
The new China.

Bibliography: p.
1. China—Description and travel—1976-
2. Beechy, Winifred. I. Title.
DS712.B43 1982 951.05 82-11800
ISBN 0-8361-3310-2 (pbk.)

PHOTO CREDITS: cover, Dwight Nissley; pages 23, 31 (two photos), 83, 101, 111, 117 (bottom), 124, 187, 215, and 250, Doug Abromski; pages 72, 74, 77, 93, 136, 142, 180, 210, 224, and 254, Atlee Beechy; pages 56, 228, and 245, Julie Froese; pages 59, 202, and 207, Cynthia Holderman; pages 117 (top), 195, 225, Robert S. Kreider; pages 55, 167, 183, Malcolm Metzler; page 84, Bruce Newswanger.

THE NEW CHINA

Published simultaneously in Canada by Herald Press, Kitchener, Ont. N2G 4M5
Library of Congress Catalog Card Number: 82-11800
International Standard Book Number: 0-8361-3310-2
Printed in the United States of America
Design by Tom Hershberger

82 83 84 85 86 87 88 10 9 8 7 6 5 4 3 2 1

To Atlee
who in our forty years
of venturing together
nudges me to do my own thing
but stands by with wise counsel
and constant support

Contents

Author's Preface

Seven hundred years ago the Venetian adventurer Marco Polo, with his merchant father and uncle, was penetrating the unknown world of the Great Khan, Khubilai, whose far-flung domain included all of today's China. After a quarter century of life and travel in the exotic world of the East, Polo's tales of all the "marvels" he had seen were related to his family and neighbors. They were fascinated by his remarkable fabrications but skeptical of any semblance to reality.

Today we know the facts of history and geography. Modern communications have closed the gap between the Oriental and the Occidental. But the movement of history in the 20th century has changed the face of China. The lavish display of wealth and waste, of pomp and power, enjoyed by the pampered imperial court has given way to the practical, survival life-style of a socialist democracy struggling to develop the riches hidden in its country's natural and personal resources. The modern Marco Polo will not find his "marvels" in jewels and cloth of gold, in feasts and hunts and battle array. He will find it in the newly awakened yearnings of the masses for a meaningful, productive life, the sense of self-reliance and determination, the willingness to sacrifice and serve, the patience and persistence of the common people, who are found to be very much akin to humanity as we find it in all the scattered dwelling places of planet earth.

This book is not intended for the China experts; they already know more than this small volume can tell of facts and figures and philosophies. It is offered as an introduction to China for the average North American reader who is seeking to rediscover the China which has been closed to us for more than 30 years. It is not the final word on the new China; it is China as I experienced it and learned of it through living in only one city and traveling a limited route. Others may see other cities and travel other routes, make different interpretations and draw different conclusions. My purpose is to give readers a feeling for the Chinese people free of myth or stereotype, an understanding of their accomplishments and hopes as well as their problems and fears, an armchair view of this vital portion of our world neighbors. I am acutely aware that what I write today may no longer be true by the time the book comes off the press so far as political and economic conditions are concerned. I hope it will still be basically true regarding the Chinese people.

My memories of China have been gleaned from lectures, field trips, experiences and interactions with Chinese people. My observations have been supplemented with readings from American and Chinese sources, classroom notes, and a personal journal. After less than 4½ months on Chinese soil, I do not claim to be a China expert and trust that you will be tolerant if I make mistakes or inadvertently give false impressions. Such errors are the responsibility of the author and not of the many people whose help I now gratefully acknowledge.

The contribution of Goshen College to this project is recognized with appreciation. The opportunity to participate in the unique exchange program was the opening of a door to the new China and the basis for a continuing interest in the Chinese "People." The friendly way in which those people opened their hearts and lives to us was a source of encouragement in my efforts to put the experience into words which might be helpful to others.

I wish to give special thanks to my husband, Atlee Beechy (professor of psychology and peace studies at Goshen College, Goshen, Indiana, and codirector of Goshen College's China Study-Service Trimester program), and to J. Winfield Fretz (former president of Conrad Grebel College and retired professor of sociology at Bethel College, North Newton, Kansas, and Conrad Grebel College, Waterloo, Ontario). Both generously read the entire manuscript and gave helpful criticism and suggestions as well as encouragement.

John S. Oyer (professor of history at Goshen College) and Gu Xue-jia (professor of history and political science at Sichuan University, currently an exchange professor of history at Goshen College), read an early draft of chapters 3 and 4. Their expert advice corrected at least some of the mistakes in the historical overview. Millard Lind (professor of Old Testament at the Associated Mennonite Biblical Seminaries, Elkhart, Indiana) read chapter 6 from a theologian's point of view, and also gave me valued advice and encouragement.

My good friend Evelyn Kreider kindly read some portions of the manuscript for general interest and readability. My three daughters deserve thanks for keeping me at work with the question they asked in every telephone conversation: "How's the book coming?" Melba Nunemaker did precise and speedy work in typing the manuscript.

Special appreciation is due Doug Abromski, who has shared his expertise and time in helping select photos for the book from the pooled collection of SST photographers. I am grateful to Goshen College Information Services for allowing access to that file, and to Doug, Julie, Cynthia, Malcolm, Bruce, and Dwight for permitting the use of their pictures. Other photos are from the collections of Atlee Beechy and Robert S. Kreider whose help is duly acknowledged.

And last, but not least, thanks to all of the 1980 China SST students through whose eyes and experiences my own understanding was broadened and enhanced.

Winifred Nelson Beechy
January 1982

Foreword

The People's Republic of China is currently hosting over one million tourists a year and the great interests in the "Middle Kingdom" remains undiminished. The vast majority of visitors stay 14 to 18 days and visit some of the major cities open to Western visitors. Housed in hotels reserved exclusively for tourists and official visitors, they travel in buses and cars provided especially for them. Their major contacts with the Chinese people are the official guides appointed to show them China's magnificent scenery, its historical sites, and the contemporary efforts to create a new society. Few return home disappointed by their experience but their impressions and knowledge of the country is obviously quite limited.

Winifred Nelson Beechy saw a different China when she and her husband Atlee accompanied 20 students from Goshen College (Indiana) on an exchange of students and faculty with the Sichuan Teachers' College at Chengdu. This city is the capitol of Sichuan, a province of 100 million people in the far west of China. For four months in 1980 she and the visiting group lived on a college campus which for several decades had been closed to Western visitors. Her endless curiosity and discerning spirit sought to enter into a deeper understanding of China's young people. Paul Rule, an Australian Jesuit, described the new China "as like living in the world's biggest religious novitiate motivated by the sense of serving people—of self-discipline for the sake of higher values."

Winifred Beechy caught the spirit of the people she met. She was fascinated, for example, with an elderly Chinese pastor who reopened the first chuch in Chengdu after all churches in the area had been closed for many years, and with other signs of spiritual awakening. (Little did she realize that two years later 220 Protestant churches would have over 1,000,000 persons attending each Sunday with 40 percent of the worshipers being under 35 years of age.)

What is it like to live on a Chinese college campus with 4,800 students and faculty? How successful was this experiment? The answer lies in the fact that Goshen College was invited to repeat the experience in 1981 and again in 1982. Reciprocating are Chinese faculty coming to Goshen College, and helping to build bridges of understanding and friendship.

I first saw Chengdu and Chungking 40 years befor Mrs. Beechy when I was there as a young missionary. As I read her interesting account I responded, "Everything has changed; nothing has changd."

Long ago Chairman Mao, the architect of the New China, with his dream of "A New Man in a New Society" wrote:

> So many deeds cry out to be done
> As always urgently
> The world rolls on;
> Time hurries;
> The thousand years are too long;
> Seize the day,
> The hour!

The New China

Today China's fourth of the world's population is dominated by this sense of urgency—impatient to modernize their nation in the closing decades of the Twentieth Century. To begin to understand the incredible dynamic of a billion people on the move, we need reliable interpreters. *The New China* will help us in that process.

J. Harry Haines, Associate General Secretary
General Board of Global Ministries
The United Methodist Church

The New China

1
Life in the Panda Palace

The daily train from Beijing, steadily and serenely making its way to Chengdu, gave no indication of the ever heightening emotions of one segment of its passenger cargo. Anticipation, curiosity, delight were all held in delicate balance with a bit of unspoken apprehension. The sun had long since set, shutting off the kaleidoscope of Chinese villages, random terraced cornfields on the mountainsides, strips of plowed earth, threshed rice drying in the sun, and bright splashes of leafy vegetables in their various shades of green. Reluctantly we drew our green velvet drapes and prepared to wait out the next few hours.

It was Tuesday, September 2, 1980—a day long circled on the calendars of at least 22 people. My husband and I were snugly settled in our first-class compartment, reminiscent of the Victorian era with its lace curtains and antimacassars (seat-back covers), its velvet window drapes, carpeted floor, and delicately shaded little table lamp. But it showed a touch of the new China in the practical thermos of hot boiled water, the covered teacups, and the shyly smiling stewardess in dark blue uniform and cap. We wondered how the 20 students bent on exploring modern China were feeling after nearly 36 hours in their economy-class coach. The Chinese government had arranged our trip, and the gap between faculty and student (or was it age and youth?) in this society was apparent. However, most of our enthusiastic troop seemed to enjoy the opportunity to mingle with the Chinese, practice their meager language skills, and listen to those Chinese who wished to practice their English.

Their accommodations were less luxurious—with clusters of six people in three-tier bunks, each equipped with a mat and a blanket and not closed off from the rest of the car. The 18 Americans and 2 Canadians became a part of the noisy confusion of the throng of Chinese travelers. Adequate though the facilities were, the lack of privacy and the blaring of broadcast music prompted some of the foreign contingent to seek out our quiet refuge occasionally. We also had visits from the three Chinese who were guiding us through this first travel experience in China. These visits kept us in touch with reality and gave us opportunity to become acquainted with our new friends. Mr. Huang was head of the foreign language department, and Miss Wang was an English teacher at Sichuan Teachers' College, our destination. Mr. Yao was from the Sichuan Province Bureau of Higher Education, the agency responsible for our being in China at all. Which takes us back to the beginning of our story.

Foreign Guests

We North Americans aboard the Beijing-Chengdu train were all from Goshen College in northern Indiana. Our college of about 1,100 students, operated by the Mennonite Church, has an international education requirement usually fulfilled by a trimester of 14 weeks in another culture, mostly countries in Latin America and the Caribbean. Students study the language, history, and culture of the host country for half the time and engage in some field experience or service project for the other half. Hence the name Study-

Service Trimester, commonly called SST.

Our college president, J. Lawrence Burkholder, with a background of relief experience in China following World War II and more recently participation with a group of educators in one of the early guided tours after China had opened her doors to such groups, thought it would be a unique experience for our students to learn something about this great and virtually unknown nation, sometimes referred to as the sleeping giant of Asia. To the surprise of all, he was able to negotiate with the Sichuan Province Bureau of Higher Education for a modified SST unit in China. Modified in that it was extended to a 16-week term because of the considerable travel expense. And modified in that it involved an exchange: Goshen College would host eight Chinese teachers of English for a period of study on its campus, and the Sichuan Bureau of Higher Education would host 20 students along with 2 faculty directors from Goshen at one of their schools. The choice fell on Sichuan Teachers' College located in Chengdu, the capital city of the province of Sichuan in south central China, an area which had been visited by few foreigners in recent years. With its 100 million people it is the largest province and one of the most productive agricultural areas in all of China.

The 20 students were selected from many hopeful applicants. My husband, Atlee, longtime professor of psychology and peace studies, and I were asked to be codirectors of the new SST unit. In preparation we all had a 3½-week elementary course in Chinese language, orientation with advice from various China experts, and preliminary contact by way of a visiting delegation, which included Mr. Huang, from "our" college in Chengdu. Atlee and I had lived in a number of Asian countries in the past and worked briefly in some others but had never been—or even dreamed of going—to China. So we boned up on books by John King Fairbank, Edgar Snow, Barbara Tuchman, and others; we sought advice on what to take and what not to take, what to do and what not to do. No one knew quite what to expect; we finally decided just to venture forth and let the chips fall where they may!

So it was that we took off from Chicago on August 25, 1980, for Beijing (Peking), the capital of the People's Republic of China (PRC). By courtesy of the airline we enjoyed an overnight stop at Tokyo's new airport, in a hotel replete with all the luxuries of the West. The next day we dropped down to the more austere atmosphere of Beijing to begin our uncharted safari in the People's Republic, our cold-war adversary for 25 years and now our sudden friend.

In describing our four-month sojourn in Chengdu, I do not wish to emphasize so much what we did there as to present the context from which we learned a little about the China of today—the sleeping giant which is awakening and stretching—and the people of China, in whose hearts there is that green bough of hope referred to in the old Chinese proverb, "If I keep a green bough in my heart, the singing bird will come."

So This Is China

On arrival in Beijing we were all impressed with the millions of bicycles (just as everyone had said we would be), with the historic treasures of the imperial past, with the friendliness and vigor of the Chinese people, with the warm welcome we received everywhere as probably the first undergraduate exchange since liberation. We were pleasantly surprised by the clean streets, the absence of beggars, the apparent good health and sound nutrition of the populace, their energetic and purposeful manner, their simple but adequate clothing. Perhaps the thing which impressed me the most was the sight of everyone carrying thermos bottles of boiled water. Knowing that impure water is the source of much disease in too many of the less developed countries, I applauded the ever present thermos—in classrooms, on trains, in the hands of truck drivers and manual laborers. What a campaign that must have been to persuade the masses to drink boiled water!

Our housing at the well-known Foreign Languages Institute did not answer all the questions which were tumbling about in our heads. "Is this what our dorm in Chengdu will be like? Will we have showers, hot water, flush toilets—Western style or Asian style?" The toilets were something new to most of our students, who promptly applied the descriptive name "squat pot." The food was delicious but somewhat westernized to please our palates. The warm, full days of sight-seeing made these typical Americans long for ice-cold drinks. But basically everything was fine, and we had made a good adjustment in this big city of Beijing. Chengdu, somewhere over the mountains in a less cosmopolitan setting, was still an unknown. After four days of the fantastic historic and scenic sights of the Beijing area, we were ready to move on. The rest and relaxation of a train trip looked especially inviting after our frantic dash to board the train following the breath-holding tie-up of our bus in a traffic jam on the way to the station. Is everyone and everything on? Sighs of relief!

Then, 36 hours later, the magic hour of 9:30 was approaching, and, sure enough, the train finished its run within five minutes of its stated arrival time. We had been told that trains run promptly on schedule in the new China, although traditionally it had not been good form to arrive too punctually for social affairs and even now the stretching of scheduled events can only be politely ignored. Our hand baggage had long been packed. At our final meal in the dining car we made our farewell speech of appreciation to the staff. In response the conductor to our great surprise presented all of us with the teacups we had been using on the trip. (These delightful souvenirs we still use when we want real Chinese tea.) I suspect we may have been the rare foreign travelers on this train, as tour groups usually do not have time for this more satisfying way of seeing the countryside.

Destination Chengdu

At last we were bundled off the train and into an obviously first-class waiting room, where we were greeted by an official welcoming committee, with whom we exchanged pleasantries by way of an interpreter while we waited for our baggage to be unloaded. Then we were off to our new home—the students in a brand-new bus to be used by the foreign student department of the college (that's us!), the mountain of baggage in a van, and the honored codirectors in a car with the director of foreign student affairs and an interpreter—plus the driver, of course.

In the People's Republic of China there are no privately owned autos. The relatively few cars are state-owned and are assigned to the use of agencies and institutions. The occupants of cars seen on the streets and highways are assumed to be government cadres on official business, foreign guests, or important personages. Each car has a chauffeur. He takes great pride in his vehicle, and during periods of waiting he constantly polishes its shining exterior and flicks the feather duster over the upholstery. Our college community of about 4,800 (plus staff families) had the use of two cars, several buses, and numerous more practical vehi-

New Chinese friends greet American visitors warmly.

cles such as trucks and construction equipment. When students are transported, it is usually by bus. Those people who do not qualify for the use of a car go by bicycle, public bus, or on foot. You will note, as we did, that the new society is very status conscious—still some distance from the classless society of the communist ideal at this point.

Our caravan made the trip to Sichuan Teachers' College, 10 kilometers (6¼ miles) from the center city, through the dark of an unknown landscape which would soon become familiar to us. We were greeted on campus by several huge banners of red bunting carrying the message—in English—"Welcome Goshen College Students." The just completed residence hall was agleam with lights and surrounded by two or three hundred students and staff, who were waiting at eleven o'clock at night to get a glimpse of their first foreign students.

Ushered into the spacious, chandelier-lighted dining hall,

we were given the customary tea and a modified welcoming ceremony. The Chinese are quite formal in this routine, with speeches by the highest-ranking official present, response by the spokesperson for the visiting group, more welcoming speeches by next-ranking personnel, appropriate response and thanks by the visitors. On the night of our arrival the ceremony was an abbreviated form since we would have our more official welcoming tea a few days later with the college president and other top administrators present. We were then served a Western-style snack of soup, sandwiches, and coffee—no doubt to make us feel at home. All the while, those several hundred pairs of eyes were looking us over through the large windows on three sides of the dining room.

Finally the festivities came to an end, and we were shown our living quarters. The students were delighted with their rooms for two, the single beds equipped with mosquito nets, warm woolen blankets, and thick comforters encased in beautifully hand-embroidered silk covers. Study tables, chairs, bookshelves, and wardrobes completed the furnishings. I'm afraid there was not too much sleeping done that first night at STC. The next few days we would get acquainted with our new home, our college, and our new friends. Our first impressions of students and staff, who were very friendly and considerate of our welfare and comfort, would be confirmed in the days and weeks ahead.

Sichuan Teachers' College

What was it like to live on a Chinese college campus? We were frankly amazed at the facilities provided for us. The new residence hall for foreign students stood out in shining splendor among the surrounding older buildings and was almost immediately christened the Panda Palace by its foreign inhabitants. The three-story stucco-over-brick building had seven student rooms on each floor, each room opening to a balcony at the back. Well-equipped bathrooms, with both Western and Asian toilets, hot and cold running water, were on each floor. Atlee and I occupied a flat on the second floor with a living room large enough for group meetings. Rooms not occupied by our SST students housed some offices and Chinese staff who watched over us, interpreted in some cases, and were generally available to help care for our needs.

Since we had been traveling for ten days, one of the first needs was laundry facilities. Clothes could be taken to a laundry in the city once a week, but it took a week for their return, so—like the Chinese students—we normally did our own. Well, not quite like the Chinese students! While we often did ours by hand, we also had available two small washing machines. The one with a spin dryer was especially popular because of difficult drying weather. The average Chinese student (or family) would depend on manual operations. Our hosts tried their best to provide us with all the luxuries to which they knew we were accustomed. We even had a TV room with a new color set. I must say that the TV got little attention from the Americans, who were more intrigued with what was going on in the world immediately around them; but the Chinese staff loved it.

Sichuan Teachers' College is located on a 70-acre campus, a city within a city at the edge of Chengdu. Most of the 3, 600 students and 1,200 faculty and staff family members live in dormitories and apartment buildings within the walled compound. It is more than an academic community; it is a cross section of humanity. Scattered among the "intellectuals" are the families of the construction workers, the maintenance people, the scores of workers who do the housekeeping chores, the merchants who provide needed supplies, the peasants who set up their fresh-produce stands at the gates and on campus.

The Panda Palace was our retreat from the strange new world in constant motion outside our fenced-in courtyard. Its superior facilities obviously discriminated in favor of the foreigners. Yet it seemed to be a source of pride, not resentment, for the Chinese students. Perhaps they saw it as a foretaste of the future, since one provincial official assured us that before too long they hoped to provide similar conveniences for all their students.

Here is our view of the campus from the Panda Palace on a typical day: From our office window we look out on a busy crossroads and watch a stream of students and staff intent on filling their thermos bottles with boiled water or carrying home bowls of food from the communal dining halls, householders shopping for meat and vegetables, students on their way to classes, or workers about their daily duties.

From the living-room window we see children, grandparents, and students taking a shortcut through our driveway, the gates of which are open during the day but closed at night. From our bedroom balcony we look down on the road which leads to the farms and small villages just outside the compound. Across this road is a large field of green leafy vegetables being harvested just minutes ahead of a construction crew. Fleets of trucks roar past hauling fill dirt to level the ground for the erection of a new faculty apartment building. We watch huge slabs of stone being unloaded and strategically placed by muscle power in close proximity to large mechanized equipment. Perhaps that is symbolic of the new China—much of the old with some of the new.

From the windowed hallway we look down on our newly

landscaped garden, which seemed to have sprouted full-grown trees and blooming flowers almost overnight. Its centerpiece—the oval pool with fountain, goldfish, and sometimes water lilies—is a magnet which draws kindergartners and primary children. Their uninhibited enthusiasm seems much like that of the children back home in North America. In the swimming pool outside our back gate, some hardy Chinese—who are used to cold showers and unheated homes—continue their polar-bear dips far into the winter.

A Walking Tour

Let's take a walk to see the rest of the campus and to get a picture of the everyday lives of our colleagues. The most interesting time, I think, is late afternoon, when classes have ended and the whole community goes into action. Whether we follow the main drives of macadam or the packed-earth footpaths in this enclave of wooded, rolling hills, we'll meet many age-groups crisscrossing the campus. Bright-eyed infants ride docilely in baskets or slings on their grandmothers' backs. Others peer out at the world from canvas prams or bamboo carriages pushed by proud fathers. Laughing pigtailed kindergartners flash past in bright flowered jackets, vivid sweaters, and gay plaid or striped pants. College students, engrossed in textbooks, read aloud as they stroll along. A dignified 80-year-old retired professor in a neat Mao jacket that is slightly too large for his shrinking figure may greet us with a surprising "Good afternoon!"

A petite, but obviously robust, young woman is digging a ditch or shoveling cement at the construction site of the new chemistry building. A patient woman wearing a gauze nose mask sweeps up the debris of littering students from the dusty streets. A worker with bulging muscles, straining between the shafts of a handcart filled with stones, inches his way up the incline of the central mall. A merchant with bicycle cart is doing a good business in noodles done up in cylindrical, open-ended packages. Near the noodle factory the long golden strands hang over wooden drying racks in the afternoon sunshine. At a nearby table a white-aproned man is cutting the noodles into prescribed lengths for packaging. Watching the operation is an old lady in blue jacket, gray pants, and black knitted cap. The ball of blue yarn unwinding from the shopping bag on her arm is rapidly taking the shape of a sweater as she visits or surveys the scene at this busy fork in the road.

A girl with black hair reaching to the bottom of her jacket pauses in the sunshine to comb her long tresses still damp from a shampoo. Some primary-school boys frisk past, their canvas schoolbags over their shoulders no deterrent to their play with frisbees or small hoops guided with bent wires. A boy with swinging jump rope has his pant legs rolled up, showing bare legs between pants and socks, while I am encased in numerous layers including long underwear and a down jacket!

Across the street a meat market is set up—a pole between two trees with eight or nine hunks of meat dangling from metal hooks. Customers make their choice; a piece is hacked off and carried away in string bag, basket, or bicycle rack. An impromptu market set up near the foreign language department office building offers green leafy vegetables, varieties of celery, and huge heads of cabbage. The large building right across the street is a faculty dining room, where families may buy various prepared foods—rice, meat toppings, vegetable dishes, steamed breads, soybean curd (dou-fu), noodles—when they choose not to cook at home. Since both men and women work outside the home, most families use this service part of the time and cook at home part of the time. It is a great convenience, but like us they consider home-cooked meals more tasty. Many of them, both men and women, enjoy cooking if they have time and facilities in their tiny apartments.

As we go down the hill, we pass office buildings, the general store, several student dining halls, student residence halls, and the central heating plant (water heating, that is). It is here that those thousands of thermos bottles are filled to be carried to dorm rooms and apartments. At certain spots on campus (in our dining hall, for example), large insulated containers of boiled water save some lucky dwellers the long trek to the heating plant. It is interesting to watch a food-service worker carrying steaming buckets of water at each end of a shoulder pole in that peculiar half-trotting gait of shoulder-pole carriers, which somehow gets them there without spills.

The central bathhouse is also located here not too far from the concentration of student dormitories, which are mostly four-story rectangles with modest rooms housing eight students each. Two double-deck beds along each wall and study tables down the center leave little space for personal belongings. Fortunately, their wardrobes require less storage space than those of most American students. These dorms are not equipped with bathrooms—hence the central bathhouse, where students are assigned times for showering. We understand that they must pay if they want warm water.

We meet students carrying brightly decorated enameled basins and plastic buckets—basic equipment for the laundering chore. Across from the two newest dorms are outdoor laundry facilities, where 12 men and women students are busily scrubbing their clothes on cement counters flanking a central drain. A water pipe with a half-dozen faucets opening to each side provides cold water. Students bring scrub brushes and soap with buckets or basins for rinsing.

A characteristic feature of the dorms is the laundry hanging dankly at all levels from bamboo poles—poles resting on outward-opening windows, poles on iron brackets below the windows, poles sticking out of windows at an angle. Clothesline strung up between two convenient trees, balcony railings of apartment buildings, even low branches of trees, are called into service for clothes drying. Our dorm has clotheslines on the flat roof of our dining room.

Keeping Fit

Right around the corner from the student dorms is the sports field. At the close of classes at 4:10 everyone promptly joins the stampede to the athletic field. Is it a natural trait, or have they been programmed by Chairman Mao's enthusiasm for building strong bodies by physical exercise? (We had the option of calisthenics or tai ji [shadowboxing] at the crack of dawn, exercises to broadcast music during the midmorning break, and more casual exercising at any between-classes break.) But the overflowing sports field in late afternoon is the sure evidence of joyful, and voluntary, participation.

Try to visualize all the activities going on at any given time. Hundreds of people out there are engaged in jogging, sprinting, impromptu badminton games, volleyball games, group calisthenics or marching drill, scheduled or casual basketball games on eight outdoor courts, individually shooting baskets or practicing volleyball serves, and a soccer team practice or game. (I always marveled that they didn't trip over each other or end up with the wrong ball in hand.)

Spectators here find added interest in the many passersby who use the field as a freeway: bicycle riders on their way to the front entrance gate; clusters of giggling girls taking a

A Chinese instructor (left) teaches tai ji, a shadowboxing morning exercise routine, to Goshen College students Maribeth Nafziger, Archbold, Ohio; Cynthia Holdeman, Lakewood, Colorado; Melody Stoltzfus, Homer, Alaska; and Julie Froese, La Junta, Colorado.

Julie Froese takes a jump shot in a coed, cross-cultural intramural game on the outdoor basketball court of Sichuan Teachers' College.

shortcut on their way home from middle school; small boys in friendly scuffles or trying their skill on the parallel bars; people going to or from the post office; parents pushing baby carriages; young matrons briskly making their way home from work, some plying bamboo knitting needles as they go; grandpas slowly toting home baskets of produce. There is no question about it; this is where the action is.

As we go back up the hill, we see several Ping-Pong games in progress on cement tables under the trees. Yes, some amateurs do play that famous game which was the prelude to the opening of the new China's door to the United States back in 1971. A bit further on we pass the shoe repairman, who has his shop set up at this strategic spot beside the pathway. He sits on a low stool, his sewing machine and supplies within reach on the ground around him, prepared to serve the needs of his customers. At the other end of the campus we find the faculty apartments, kindergarten, primary school, and outdoor theater. Small flower gardens and potted plants frequently show evidence of "green thumbs." The back gate opens to fruit orchards, a favorite place for evening walks or shopping at the free market.

Time for Supper

By this time the supper hour has arrived, and we see students with bowls and chopsticks on their way to pick up some food at the dining hall. They may take it to their rooms or eat as they stand about, squat on their heels in the company of friends, or walk along. Small children sometimes eat as they sit on their doorsteps or play with friends in the street. Students provide their own utensils and do their own dishwashing.

Behind our new residence hall is a row of faucets above a

narrow, counterlike trough intended for washing our dishes. But the system was not inaugurated for us. Special meal service was provided for us in the Panda Palace, where our cooks prepared our fixed menu, served us at small tables, and did the dishwashing. Our Chinese hosts took this measure to safeguard our health from the digestive upsets that newcomers to Asia usually suffer; they feared that our students could not tolerate the hot spicy foods of Sichuan and were even prepared to give us so-called American-style cooking. There was some disappointment among our students at being segregated. Most of us took well to the Sichuan food and were soon shunning the offer of Western cooking, except for the solace of that familiar piece of toast at breakfast time. By the end of our stay some of the group were occasionally eating with friends in the communal dining halls as well as from the street-side stalls in the city, their once sensitive digestive systems having built up some resistance to the new "bugs" which had at first upset them. From the soapsuds and boiling-water rinse which we take for granted, we had adjusted to the soapless and cold-water dishwashing common to many Asian countries.

Rules and Regulations

Our daily routine conformed to the campus schedule, which in turn followed the pattern of all colleges and universities in China at this time. When our students were enrolled as special students at Sichuan Teachers' College, they were formally read (in Chinese and English) all the rules and regulations which they were expected to observe along with their Chinese counterparts: Visitors are not allowed in the dorms; a visitor from off campus must have a pass to be admitted at the entrance. Students must show their I.D. cards to leave or return to campus. They are expected to leave the classroom buildings at 10:00 p.m. and have lights out in the dorms at 11:00 p.m. A student who misses more than one day of class must have a doctor's permit to re-enter. Normally students are not expected to make trips into the city except on Saturday afternoons and Sundays, when classes are not in session. (The college bus makes a number of trips on each of these days. The city bus stop is a walk of about one mile from campus.)

Add to all of this a few protective measures for foreigners. If they left campus, our students were expected to return before dark. They were cautioned to walk in twos outside the compound and, better yet, to take along a Chinese friend. The reason given: "Even in a socialist society there are still some bad elements." Our students were asked not to ride bicycles off campus because of the hazards of unfamiliar traffic patterns. (I was secretly relieved at this order!)

Our American students were quite taken aback by what they considered very strict regimentation. Older memories could recall some similar restrictions in our own colleges 40 to 50 years ago. Of course, there are always ways of circumventing the rules. We soon noted that the Chinese students were not always in the dorms by 10:00 and dorms were often still lighted up after 11:00. But certainly control is much more stringent than on American campuses. Most students are required to live on campus; they are not allowed to get married until after graduation; they are not free to drop in or out of college at will or to switch courses as their interests change. Being chosen as one of the select few who may attend college is a great privilege, and their future careers depend upon making the most of the opportunity.

At STC there is a chiming bell for rising, for doing exercises, for going to class, for beginning and ending class, for meals, for "self study" (students go to classrooms to study in the evenings), for returning to the dorms, and for bedtime. The campus is equipped with a loudspeaker system, which can be heard in the farthest corners—even if you put your cotton-padded comforter over your head! The 6:00 a.m. chime marks the time for rising and is followed by announcements, news, and music. By 6:30 the early birds are out for tai ji and other forms of exercise to the broadcast music. Throughout the day the loudspeakers announced our meals, work, rest, play, and more news, until the final familiar signal proclaimed the end of another day.

Days of Work and Study

Our program called for three hours of intensive Chinese language study each day during the first three weeks and one hour daily for the rest of the term. We were given a total of 60 hours of lectures on history and culture, economics, politics, literature, music, and art. On Saturdays and Sundays we were taken on a total of 20 field trips to scenic or historic places, handicraft workshops, communes, and factories. After the first five weeks our students began their service assignment, which was to help teach English in the foreign language department. About 250 Chinese were studying English in preparation for teaching it in the middle schools (comparable to our high schools).

Remarkable progress had been made without the aid of native English-speaking teachers for these many years. But students and faculty alike were looking forward to the coming of these young foreigners who would teach them not only American English but also about American culture and life-styles, about which they had an insatiable curiosity. Our students were swamped with young Chinese who wished to practice their English and make friends with Americans since the Chinese and American governments had decided that we could again be friends and that our Western science and technology would help the PRC achieve its goals of full modernization by the year 2000.

It was a unique opportunity for cross-cultural exchange and one which our students thoroughly enjoyed after they overcame the trauma of actually being put in charge of a classroom. They spent many hours each day with their classes, in structured sessions and informal activities. They were taken on shopping tours, on picnics, to visit in homes, to athletic and entertainment events. Through compositions and class discussions they learned much about the "system," recent history, home life, the hopes and fears regarding an uncertain future. They learned—as everyone should know—that socialists, communists, and capitalists are all human beings with aspirations and dreams which have more commonalities than differences.

Some Fun Times Too

Frequently the evening study period would be scuttled by the showing of a film. Then the street would be filled with students carrying their stools or chairs, all headed in the direction of the open-air theater. The Chinese seem to love movies and especially the foreign ones from Japan, England, or the United States. While the PRC makes quite a few films, they often have had a propagandistic or moralistic tone, at least in the judgment of Westerners. With the new moderate trend in government, there is hope that more creativity will be allowed in this medium. Films in English are prized by the language students as an opportunity to practice listening comprehension. One of the few movies I attended was the English classic *Great Expectations*. In this case—you guessed it—the dialogue was in Chinese!

Aside from movies, which are partly educational, what

else do students do for entertainment? Students take initiative for providing a good bit of their own entertainments—singing, drama, classical dance, readings, skits, instrumental music (both Western and traditional). They also enjoy opera and musical programs by professionals. The classical dance dramas which were in ill repute with all the other "olds" during the Cultural Revolution are again acceptable.

Local talent programs always had a female announcer who wore a long Western-style dress, preferably white, and rather heavy makeup. A somewhat stilted, artificial voice with a singsong quality was characteristic of all announcers, whether amateur or professional. The theatrical makeup seemed garish in contrast to the cosmetic-free complexions in daily life. I wondered whether this might not be a carryover from the traditional opera, in which the stylized makeup indicates the character of the roles portrayed—certain colors and designs for the good guys, others for the bad guys, for example. In any case, students seemed to have a lot of fun preparing and presenting these entertainments.

Long Underwear and Fleece-lined Boots

Because of our hothouse upbringing one of our more difficult adjustments was to unheated buildings. While the Sichuan basin has a temperate climate, with no snow and rarely frost, it can be quite chilly in the fall and winter, especially for those accustomed to heated houses, vehicles, and public buildings. In November and December, when the thermometer in our living room hovered around 48 to 52 degrees Fahrenheit, it became quite a challenge to keep comfortable. We learned to compensate with four or five layers of clothing and cups of hot tea or hot water. We came home to our overheated house in Indiana and turned our thermostat down to 60. But we found we were misfits in our own society; we had to keep sweaters or afghans handy for shivering friends who came to call improperly dressed for our indoor climate. They hadn't learned the secret of long underwear!

Chengdu friends often apologized for their climate and the lack of sunshine. There is an old Chinese saying which tells the story, "... rare as a Sichuan dog barking at the sun." But when the sun did shine, it was beautiful and exhilarating to be outdoors. Much depends on acculturation. North Americans in down jackets and wool mittens would go to the classroom and close all the windows. The lecturer would come in and throw the windows wide open; the interpreter kept a handkerchief handy to wipe the perspiration from her brow.

A Place of Retreat

In retrospect, life in the Panda Palace had its routine moments and its high moments. It is too demanding to live constantly in a state of elation. The Panda Palace became a place of refuge—a place to get away from the crowds and recoup one's physical and emotional energy; its inhabitants were a support group who understood the cultural shock of the thrilling, but sometimes daunting, new experience.

Individualistic Western travelers, with high regard for privacy, find it a problem to cope with the intense interest and curiosity inspired by the unfamiliar sight of foreign visitors. Blondes and redheads, blue eyes and fair skins, bright jackets and slacks of a different cut—all stand out in the crowds of black-haired, dark-eyed Chinese in their somewhat uniform clothing of modest design and color. Even after we became a familiar sight on campus, we attacted much attention on shopping or field trips. Whenever our bus stopped, even before the first passenger set foot to the ground, it seemed to be a signal to halt traffic—pedestrian and bicycle—and we were soon the center of a circle of people who stared after us as we walked down the street and into the shops. No hostility, just pure curiosity and amazement at the foreigners, a desire to see how they dressed, how they talked, what they were going to buy. Sometimes the bolder ones, trying out their English, would ask questions or offer help. Their curiosity was friendly, to be sure, but at times almost overwhelming.

It felt good to get back to the security of the Panda Palace. There we were just one of the crowd, and no one invaded our privacy. Of course, from our safe retreat we less straightforwardly continued to stare out at "them," to see how they dressed, how they talked, what they were going to buy! But this was all a part of the education and enhanced understanding for which we had come to China. We owe many thanks to our Chinese student and faculty friends who helped us to process and assimilate the unfamiliar sights, sounds, tastes, feelings, and facts presented to us in the context of the Sichuan Teachers' College community and the surrounding city and province.

A Tearful Parting

The four months on the STC campus and in transit were an intensive learning experience, which we relived and integrated at a more leisurely pace as we made our way by riverboat down the mighty Yangtze in late December. The final parting of Chinese and American students late at night at the Chengdu railroad station had been a highly emotional moment. Real friendships had been planted, and the uprooting was more difficult than anyone could have dreamed. Through the total interchange, decidedly different individuals were leaving Shanghai on Christmas day from the ones who had entered Beijing just four months earlier. We have reason to believe that the cross-cultural enlightenment was mutual. While the results will not be earthshaking, we feel confident that our life in the Panda Palace will contribute in some small measure to the international understanding so much needed in our small world of today. The view from windows slightly ajar call for further opening and exploration.

2
We Meet the People

In a People's Republic it is only natural that one hears a great deal about "the people"—National People's Congress, People's Liberation Army, people's currency, People's Publishing House, people's communes, people's parks, and so on and on. Who are these people? How do they look, dress, eat, work, play, make their homes, and organize their daily lives? First, I would like you to meet a few of the people we came to know and appreciate.

One Billion Individuals

Meet Mr. Huang, dean of the foreign language department of our college, with his excellent English and a consoling understanding of the ways of Westerners. He and his beautiful wife, Shih, who teaches Russian, were the first to extend friendship and persons whom we could freely ask our many questions. Meet the other Mr. Huang, who was our guide and interpreter on many field trips. He had translated into vernacular English the works of Lu Xun, a famous revolutionary poet. His extensive use of American idioms was a source of enjoyment, amusement, and sometimes embarrassment, leading us to suspect he had picked up some expressions from American soldiers.

Meet Mr. Nie, our low-key but extremely adept Chinese-language teacher, who spoke no English but, after one day with an interpreter, communicated the intricacies and meanings of Chinese script. His sparkling smile of encouragement gave the hesitant courage to try again. Meet Miss Wang, petite and youthful English teacher, who shared our lives as interpreter, liaison person, and expediter. Her diminutive frame packed a big muscle, first displayed at Beijing airport when she briskly grabbed two big suitcases and proceeded to help load the baggage onto the waiting bus. Meet handsome Mr. Zhao, director of foreign student affairs, who with long-suffering vice-director Zhang in charge of our dorm, spent many hours in our apartment diplomatically drinking tea and exchanging pleasantries before getting down to some mistake or misconduct of one of our brood, or sharing plans for some new venture.

Meet another Mr. Zhang, vice-president of Sichuan Teachers' College, who cheerfully exchanged banter with me (if that was possible with the few words of Chinese I could muster) about his three sons and my three daughters. Perhaps he saw me as a fellow sinner because I, too, had more than the accepted one or two offspring. Meet efficient Miss Lu, whose coherent interpretations kept us informed of official policy and daily events. Her husband was one of the few Chinese I saw wearing a hearing aid, hence some feeling of empathy although my aid was more modern than his. Meet Mr. Yao from the Bureau of Higher Education, whose hobbies were sketching lovable panda bears and studying English, which he practiced on us during our 30-hour train trip to Guangzhou (Canton), having risen to the unexpected communication task when at the last minute Miss Wang was unable to go.

Meet spunky old Professor Sen, who had studied at two great American universities in his youth and wore an old-fashioned beard, bringing Red Guard harassment during the Cultural Revolution. His spunkiness, his beard, and his American connection probably all contributed to his mistreatment. Twice the Red Guards forcibly cut off his beard; twice he let it grow again. The third time, he says, he put his foot down and told them, "If you cut off my beard, cut off my head!" He still has his beard and his independent spirit along with a vast knowledge of American history, world history, and Chinese history.

I could go on; there is no good cutoff place. I do not wish to slight any of the scores of people who contributed to our enjoyment and enlightenment. But there are a billion other Chinese out there, and you should have a general introduction to them.

Their Clothing Is Similar

Chinese people are as impossible to describe in generalities as are North Americans. One may safely say they have black hair and dark eyes with that distinctive Oriental shape. After that, they come in various packages. It is not completely true that they are all short and of slight build; many are, but they also come in tall, stocky, or average sizes. Fat ones are very rare. Some are handsome, some are not; some have straight hair, some have curly hair. Clothing conforms to a uniform model much more than individuals do. In fact, first impressions confirmed our concept of a socialist society as an egalitarian one, in which class or economic distinctions are de-emphasized and a simple lifestyle is the norm. On city streets, on campuses, at tourist attractions and cultural events, we noted the undeviating sameness of costume among both men and women.

Invariably, the men wear the slightly baggy trousers topped with dark blue, green, or gray Mao jackets. Sport-type shirts worn over the trousers are unencumbered with a tie. The Mao jackets buttoned to the neck with fold-down collar revealing the top edge of shirt collars are reminiscent of the clerical collars of our own church's recent past. A simple zippered jacket is an alternative. The more sophisticated professional men who put on coat and tie to travel to the West, revert to regulation garb back on their home turf.

The only clue to status may be the shoes—the more sturdy leather shoes of the teacher or government official, the sneakers or leather sandals of students, the rubber sandals or plastic boots of the women and men on construction jobs. But there is no clear-cut distinction. Shoes made of cloth are very popular, although they don't look very serviceable. Many of our students bought them and found them comfortable. I even saw them on the feet of a peasant woman working with us in the muddy clay of a commune field.

Women apparently need spend little time on fashion or shopping for original garments. Like the men, they wear the baggy pants of the liberation era with simple cotton blouses in a variety of prints or plain colors. The basic boxy, three- or four-button jacket, in a somewhat greater variety of colors and materials than those worn by men, completes the outfit. Mao jackets are popular with them also, especially among the young. The net effect should be to make that daily decision of what to wear a simple and uncomplicated one. (I more or less adopted the interchangeable-two-outfits routine myself!)

In the larger, more cosmopolitan cities, Western influences are more evident; in Beijing we occasionally saw women in dresses and little girls decked out in frills and ruffles. Summertime brings out more skirts and dresses. In the winter, except in the South, there is a change to warm seasonal garments—fur- or fleece-lined shoes; long underwear; hand-knitted sweaters, caps, and mittens; and bulky cotton-padded jackets or coats. Cotton-padded garments have washable removable covers, as did the cotton-filled comforters on our dormitory beds.

In any crowd young men and women in bright army-green uniforms stood out, their Mao jackets displaying a red rectangle on each flap of the collar and their caps a red star. These markings, by the way, did not indicate rank. The People's Liberation Army does not make this distinction in the uniform at the present time.

Free from Old Customs and New Fashions

Drives through the countryside reveal a few old men still wearing really baggy pants under longish coats and women wearing the side-closing mandarin-collar jackets with "frog" loop closures of the old China. Remnants of foot-binding days remain in the shuffling walk and tiny feet of some of the little old ladies. But in clothing the old is not admired now. Only in small villages or on very old people does one see any signs of the traditional garb. In fact, some of our students, intrigued by these styles which looked more "Chinese," bought materials for jackets or blouses and had great difficulty finding a tailor who was willing to make them up. Modern Chinese reject the elegance and discomfort of the past for the simplicity and functionalism of the new China. Only shops for tourists display luxury fabrics fashioned into traditional jackets or gowns.

Most women use no makeup, and one sees very few articles of jewelry. There are decorative pins, mostly the popular Chinese-American friendship pins with miniature flags of the PRC and the United States—also some with slogans promoting patriotic campaigns. (The commonly worn identification badge bearing the name of one's institution or workplace hardly rates as jewelry.) During the long years of the revolutions, the use of cosmetics or jewelry was frowned upon as signs of bourgeois or capitalist decadence. Straight, bobbed hair and braids are standard hairdos, but today many young women do patronize the beauty parlors, and some come out with curly hair. A young friend, faithful to the socialist ideal and very attractive at any rate in her straight, bobbed hair, scorned the frivolity of a permanent.

Most people are very neat in their personal appearance, even those in patched clothing, but do not seem to be preoccupied with it. Women and men are concerned about the cut and fit of their garments. When Westerners use the term "baggy pants," it is only a relative term; our tight-fitting pants styles of today may rotate to the more loosely fitted ones tomorrow. Whether the simplicity and uniformity of dress is inspired by economics or patriotism, is not clear. Perhaps both. I personally found it refreshing to see people oblivious to fashion designers' conniving, Madison Avenue-type pressures, and commercial sales chart influences. The increase in consumer goods, the intensifying of westernizing influences, and a corresponding lessening of political education against immoral capitalist practices may change all this in a short time. Clothing is already much more colorful and varied than it was a few years ago.

What Do They Eat?

The food of the people hardly needs to be discussed because of the availability of Chinese restaurants in every corner of the world. To the plentiful supply of Chinese restaurants in the United States offering Mandarin, Peking, or Cantonese cuisine has in recent years been added the Sichuan (Szechwan) restaurants with their generous use of red-hot chili peppers. While the old familiar fried rice, Peking duck, wonton soup, stir-fried vegetables, soybean curd (doufu), and egg rolls are on Chinese menus, I hope you won't be too disappointed to learn that the food in China is not quite like that at your favorite Golden Dragon or Shanghai Gardens. Chinese restaurants around the world (and they are around the world) tend to take on the flavor of their host countries' cooking.

Most of our group became very fond of the hot and spicy food, even the great variety of dou-fu (each region claims its own as superior), and quite adept at the use of chopsticks. Bringing a slippery tidbit from a serving dish in the center of the big round banquet table to your own rice bowl can be quite a test. Foods are never passed, but your Chinese neighbors may keep filling your bowl with more than you ever thought you wanted.

Like people here at home, we enjoyed three meals a day. Our basic breakfast consisted of rice gruel; mantou (a steamed bread much like our steamed dumplings) or toast; sometimes a pickled vegetable, which invariably remained on the table at the end of the meal; hot tea or hot milk. Eggs were offered to us in the early days, a concession to perceived American practice. That was eventually given up; the one touch of home which we held onto was the toast and jam. It had been something of a security blanket for slightly queasy stomachs in the early days, and we continued to depend on it.

Our main meal at noon settled down to rice with three or four side dishes of vegetables and/or meat, ending with soup. Meat is chopped into small pieces and used to season the various vegetable dishes, which in the fall means varieties of celery, onions, cabbages, leafy greens, cauliflower, sometimes potatoes and sweet potatoes. Supper consisted of rice again with two side dishes, or noodles with a spicy meat topping. You will note that we had a very adequate diet, largely without desserts.

At festive or banquet-type meals the Chinese may serve as many as 15 to 20 different dishes (courses), beginning with cold meats and ending with soup or noodles. On such occasions a fresh fruit or sweet soup may be included. Sweets and fruits are more likely to be a part of the diplomatic or celebrative tea parties on important occasions.

The Chinese tea usually offered to us was what our hosts called "flower tea" (jasmine in leaf form). The tea leaves are steeped in covered cups with hot water from a thermos. As the program/class/conversation progresses, you occasionally take a sip. Ideally, the leaves settle to the bottom, but if they refuse, you simply strain the beverage through your teeth. After a time someone will refill the cup with hot water; they say the second brewing is more tasty than the first. It is a convenient way to serve tea—no sugar, milk, or lemon to complicate the serving; and the delicate flavor is not distorted.

Our diet, it must be remembered, was more lavish than the average Chinese diet. Funds allocated for our students' food were 45 yuan per month compared to 17 yuan for the Chinese students. That figures out to one U.S. dollar per day for Americans and only about 40 cents per day for the Chinese. I suspect that the variety of dishes, the amount of meat, and the fact that our meals were not mass-produced in the communal dining halls account for the difference. Chinese people, in general, look well fed and healthy. Although certain foods are still rationed—cooking oil, rice and wheat products—there is an adequate supply in most areas. Admittedly, some malnutrition still exists in less productive and remote areas, but people are not dying of starvation as in the "bad old days."

Chinese families must spend a higher proportion of their income on food than we do even with current inflation. Worker families in one of the large cities in 1980 spent 53 percent of their total wages on food; this compared favorably to 70 percent back in 1965. Chengdu is in the center of one of the most fruitful agricultural areas in China and enjoys a bountiful supply of vegetables, meat products, cereal grains, and fruits. When one stops to consider that less than 15 percent of the land of that sprawling nation must supply food for its billion hungry people, it seems a spectacular feat.

Houses Are Modest

What kinds of houses do the people call home? New construction is much in evidence across China, but there is still a severe shortage of housing. It seems impossible for housing to catch up with demand following the long years of war and the phenomenal growth in population. Buildings are mainly of brick, stone, or cement—many times with a stucco finish. They produce a somewhat drab landscape for those of us who are accustomed to the bright touches of color in painted wooden buildings. Peasants build small cottages of adobe or mud and sometimes with plastered panels of woven bamboo, framed with exposed timbers. Thatched or tile roofs add an exotic touch.

Urban dwellers live predominantly in apartment buildings or the old-style row houses within walled compounds. Multiple-family dwellings are the general rule; land is a critical factor, and every inch of productive soil must be utilized for food production. Homes are rarely privately owned; housing is allocated by the workplace (factory, commune, institution) or government unit. Peasants continue to live in their ancestral, single-family homes even though technically they are owned by the collective.

Apartments are small by our standards. The concept of a "living room" is something that needs explanation. Most homes cannot afford the luxury of one room used exclusively as a living room; each room serves a dual function as bedroom/living room, bedroom/study, bedroom/dining room, or all of these combined. The furnishings of most rooms include a bed. One of the roomiest homes we visited had a study/living room combination without a bed, but it did serve as dining room for our party of eight around the meter-square table carried in for the occasion. The parents' bedroom, equipped with several wicker chairs and a small TV set, also served as living room. This was the home of a father, mother, and three sons—two of them still at home. The boys' bedroom, a tiny kitchen, and a bathroom completed the living space.

Many families occupy only one or two rooms plus a small kitchen, sharing bathroom facilities with other apartments on the same floor. Housing assignments are supposedly made according to the needs of each family. Single men or women may be housed in a dormitory-type arrangement. Life in the countryside is similarly characterized by economy of space. A peasant woman on a commune proudly showed us the simple home occupied by her family. A cluster of small buildings arranged around an open courtyard provided living and sleeping space in two or three rooms in one wing. A detached kitchen, toilet, storage room, and pig shed were in adjacent buildings. The living wing was neatly arranged with embroidered comforter covers and decorative valances over the beds. Picture calendars and family snapshots hung on walls papered with newspapers. No cozy rugs adorned the hard-packed mud floor, but a few books and a pot of flowers on the small table, along with the everpresent thermoses, added a homey touch.

The size or elegance of the home does not always indicate the quality of life within its walls. At the simple two-room apartment of a professor friend, we were impressed by the range of reading materials on his bookshelves, both Chinese and English, professional and general. Another professor's living room/study proclaimed his interest in the Chinese classics through a collection of well-worn books. Artistic scrolls of calligraphy adorned the cement wall. When he brought out a precious Ming pottery bowl for our inspection, I hesitated to hold in my hands this antique treasure. Imagine our surprise to be served apples from it!

Geography Affects Lifestyle

China has always been an intriguing place. Remember when you were a youngster digging in the sand and believing that if you could go deep enough you'd uncover China on the other side of the planet? Indeed North America is just about opposite China on the top half of the globe. Situated in the middle of the Asian continent, it is a sprawling giant, the third largest country in the world after Canada and the USSR, and just ahead of the United States. Parts of it stretch north to south as far as from Manitoba to Haiti, giving it a variety of climates and vegetation from its tropical South to the windswept, snow-chilled North.

This great nation displays an endless variety of terrain—broad fertile plains, rolling hills, high plateaus, huge deserts, vast expanses of grassland, steep and rugged mountains. The panorama of its beauties ranges the full spectrum from the lush tropical greens to the gray-brown hues of desert and grazing lands to awesome and majestic mountain peaks, mysterious in veils of mist or snow.

Aside from its huge landmass it has other big dimensions. Its coastline measures 3,600 miles, and the extremely long land boundary of 17,000 miles separates it from a full dozen next-door neighbors. Mount Qomolangma (Everest), the highest peak in the world, towers over the "roof of the world" on the Nepal border. The mighty Changjiang (Yangtze) is the largest river in Asia, third largest in the world. The famous 2,200-year-old Dujiangyan Irrigation System waters more than a million of Sichuan's fertile acres. Finally, China's one billion people give it the largest population on earth. Imagine a procession of the world's people. Every fourth person filing past would be an inhabitant of the People's Republic of China (not to mention the millions of Chinese who live in many other countries).

Where do all these people live? Since 80 to 85 percent of them are still engaged in the tasks of food production, a large majority of them live in the rural areas. But only 12 to 15 percent of China's landmass is cultivable; this means that farmlands support highly concentrated populations. In a rich farming area such as Sichuan Province, population density may reach 3,300 per square mile of cropland. In the nation overall, 95 percent of the people are crowded onto 45 percent of the land area.

An outstanding characteristic of the Chinese population is its youthfulness. In 1977 only 17.5 percent of the people were over the age of 45. (What a bonanza that would be for the U.S. Social Security System!) Almost half were under the age of 18. The most populous age-groups were the 5- to 15-year-olds (24.9 percent) and the 15- to 25-year-olds (20.2 percent) *[Encyclopedia of China Today]*. Another way of stating this unusual situation is that 86 percent are below age 50, and 40 percent below 18 years of age *(The Times Atlas of China)*.

Following the founding of the PRC, there was a bulge in birth rates encouraged by the expectation of speedy industrialization and demand for a large labor force. Another upsurge in births occurred during the Cultural Revolution (1966-1976), when family planning was looked upon as a bourgeois conspiracy to control the common people. Between 1950 and 1980, population figures increased about 80 percent, crossing the one billion mark in 1980—one quarter of the globe's total.

Ethnic Origins

What kinds of people make up this great mass of humanity? The Han Chinese, who are the basic ethnic group, make up 94 percent of the total. The Chinese had their beginnings in the Yellow River basin and spread out over the central and eastern plains. The name Han was taken from the Han dynasty, which ruled from 206 BC to 220 AD. Other ethnic groups around the edges of Han settlements were absorbed by the Han. Groups more recently incorporated into the empire are known as national minorities. These non-Han minorities consist of 55 ethnic or tribal groups, which today number close to 60 million and make up the remaining six percent of the population.

The minorities are not strictly segregated; some Hans live in the same areas. The regions which have major concentrations of minority groups take up more than half of the country's territory. They live in the very sparsely settled desert, grassland, or mountain regions; some are still seminomadic. The Hans tend to be concentrated in the more productive areas, the less than half of the country which is considerably overpopulated. The 55 minorities differ from the Han majority in one or more of the following: language, customs, religion, race, or historical background. Their groups vary in size from over 12 million to only 600.

The government has adopted policies generally favorable to the minorities. For example, they are given limited autonomy to manage their own affairs; they are provided special educational and training programs; they are allowed to keep their native languages, customs, and religions; they are given economic and other development assistance; and they are exempted from the national birth control campaigns, which are being conducted quite rigorously among Han Chinese. The benefits are claimed to be part of the effort to gain support for the "united front" appraoch, recruitment of all segments of the nation to contribute to building the new socialist society. In theory the policies sound quite ideal. In practice, one might get a different picture from minority persons themselves, depending on how national policies are administered in local regions.

It should be mentioned here that the PRC is divided into 30 administrative units (equivalent to our states): 22 provinces, 5 autonomous regions, and 3 municipalities. The three largest cities—Shanghai with 12 million people, Beijing with 8½ million, and Tianjin (Tientsin) with 7 million—have provincial status in relation to the central government. Many of the major concentrations of ethnic minority groups live in the autonomous regions.

Communication in an Ancient Language

How do all the people communicate with each other in this enormous nation? The Chinese language is one which poses some problems for Westerners. But for the Chinese it provides one common element for the widespread populace. The unphonetic, nonalphabetic characters which form its unique script, link modern Chinese with their ancestors and with their far-flung peers. The Chinese characters are written the same way and have the same meaning across the nation. But since they are not phonetic, speakers pronounce them differently in the hundreds of regional dialects, making oral communication a problem. The new China's national language, putonghua, is a simplified form of the northern dialect often referred to as Mandarin because it was the official language of the imperial scholar-administrators called mandarins. Putonghua is taught in Chinese schools and used by most educated people as their first or second language along with the local dialect.

The Chinese characters, symbols which carry the meaning of words or ideas, must each be learned as we who use the roman alphabet must learn the ABC's. A reader of newspapers or ordinary books should know at least 2,000—a more literate person needs 3,000—of the total 60,000 characters. General-purpose dictionaries list perhaps 7,000.

In spite of the cumbersome language, by the year 1750 more books had been published in Chinese than in all other languages of the world together. Of course, the Chinese had

Chinese women help American Maria Glick with her language study.

Curious Chinese watch American student Mark Liechty buy peanuts from curbside market.

invented paper and printing centuries before Europeans used them.

Foreign learners of Chinese find it difficult to master the intricate script and the tonal quality of the language. We may translate the script into its roman equivalent, but one must be careful to use the proper tone of voice. Four tonal accents give different meanings to words that are exactly the same in romanized form. For example, the common word "ma" has four possible meanings depending on the tone of voice. One means horse; one means mother-in-law. I can't remember the others, but you can see how easily a speaker can get into deep trouble! Or take the word "Mao" as in Mao Zedong; it is also the word for cat in a different tone. The unwary, by the slip of a tone, may be guilty of calling Chairman Mao a cat.

Some feel that the language has limited China's interaction with the outside world and are predicting that romanized script will someday replace the characters which have been in use for over 3,000 years. The desire for modernization may give impetus to such a move (you can't have a 60,000-key typewriter, and you can't transmit characters by teleprinter), but if it happens it will be a very gradual process. Language is a vital part of a nation's identity and closely entwined with its roots. Calligraphy, beautiful handwritten script, is one of China's traditional art forms still popular today.

Work and Play

Where the people go for their working hours will be considered further when we look at the economic system. But a simple overview would show that between 80 and 85 percent of them are engaged in some sort of agricultural pursuit. The rest are involved in such things as industry, education, health care, construction, research, public service, and government administration; but whatever their occupations, they are basically all employees of the same "boss" since all these enterprises are under state control and state ownership. Most of the agricultural workers, on the other hand, are members of communes which are collectively owned although regulated by the state.

While the Chinese give the impression of being an energetic, hardworking people, they also take some time for recreation. One has only to visit a park, pagoda, or other scenic/historic spot any day of the week to be persuaded of their love for a holiday or family outing. Since work goes on seven days a week at many jobs, days off are staggered and any day can produce crowds just as a special holiday weekend does here in the United States. There is much picnicking, posing for camera fans, sampling of sweets and amusements at the parks and folk fairs. Groups take excursions by bicycle, bus, truck, or train to such popular recreation sites.

We've already noted their love for movies. Sports events, mountain climbing, music and dance programs, acrobatics, and opera all draw crowds. Regional opera companies through the years have developed their unique styles of performance. Beijing Opera and Shanghai Opera are best known because of their occasional foreign tours, but Chengdu has its own Sichuan Opera with roots far in the past also. During the Cultural Revolution the "powers that be" restricted the repertoire to patriotic and revolutionary themes, but now opera companies again perform the old classical favorites, which are no longer stigmatized by association with the feudal past.

Many ancient festivals are gaily and colorfully celebrated, including New Year's Day and the Lantern Festival in the winter and the Flower Festival in the spring—festivals related to the changing seasons and the high points of the life cycle. Such festivals, based on historical events or mythology, often feature family gatherings and special feasts. For example, the Dragon Boat Festival in midsummer celebrates the memory of a patriotic poet of the third century BC who supposedly drowned himself after learning that the capital city had fallen to the enemy. Families prepare a traditional delicacy, the food which—according to the folktale—was thrown into the river to dissuade the dragons from eating the poet's body.

Such festivals, along with national holidays, still play a role in forming a cohesive society. Even the patriotic fervor of "serving the people" and building the ideal socialist society must allow for an occasional break just to relax and have a good time. The constitution, after affirming the citizen's right to work, declares that working people have the right to rest (article 49). To ensure this right the state prescribes working hours and systems of vacations providing such rest periods. Workers look forward to vacations each year, when they can go on more extended trips—traveling to other cities to visit relatives, hiking in the mountains, or touring favorite memorial sites.

Living Standards

Americans ask us about the living standards of the people. Research on workers' families in a major city in 1980 gives us some statistics based on three representative families: a well-off family, a middle-income family, and a low-income family ("Workers' Living Standards in Tianjin," *China Reconstructs*, July 1981). The major difference was not in salary earned but in the number of working members in each family. While monthly salaries of the workers in these

Thousands of bicycles crowd the streets of China's cities.

three families ranged only from 60 yuan to 81 yuan, the per capita income ranged from about 23 to 68 yuan. Perhaps this explains why most wives and mothers are expected to work outside the home. Housing did not vary greatly. The well-off family had a two-room apartment, the other two only one-room apartments, plus kitchen and bath facilities.

The per capita income of the 500 families (all factory employees) was about 40 yuan per month (equal to $27 in the United States). In spite of the low pay level, the number of consumer goods owned was relatively high; for every 100 families there were 185 bicycles, 71 sewing machines, 249 wristwatches (it seemed to me that everyone had a wristwatch!), 110 radios, 54 TV sets, 6 tape recorders, nearly 5 cameras, 18 electric fans, and 22 pairs of easy chairs. Since we are prone to measure living standard by consumer goods, this gives us some idea of what working people are able to do with their relatively few yuan. When we look at communes, we shall see that peasant families generally have a much lower cash income.

On the professional level, living standards are higher. I can cite the example of one young teacher friend. As a beginning teacher her salary was 60 yuan per month ($40). She had recently married a young medical doctor, who earned 100 yuan per month. The workplace customarily assigns housing, and since they work for separate institutions ten kilometers apart, she kept her dormitory room and commuted to his small apartment only once or twice a week.

Rents are very low; a small apartment might include electricity and water for a charge of only several yuan a month. Another teacher friend told me that he and his wife spend only 3 percent of their combined 230-yuan monthly income for rent and utilities. Food takes a much larger share. The young woman teacher spends close to half of her earnings for food, mostly from the college food services. The couple do their own cooking on weekends except when they go to visit her parents, quite regularly on Sundays. Clothing is not a large item, nor are household furnishings for a small apartment. They are able to put savings in the bank each month from their combined salaries of just over $100 (U.S.).

What do Chinese families save for since neither houses nor cars can be privately owned? More consumer goods are becoming available. They save for a TV set, a radio, a tape recorder, books, art objects, vacations, and possibly for that one- or two-child family. The advent of a child will bring down their per capita income for some years. Young people in China, like human beings everywhere, look forward to a more comfortable, more fulfilling life for themselves and their society.

Cultural Differences

So, we learned about the people and from the people. Their friendliness and openness, and our feelings of mutuality with them, made our sojourn in a foreign land memorable. But one must be aware of cultural differences.

Just as there are differences among individuals, there are cultural differences; and the alien resident must learn to accept and respect such differences. For instance, in our privacy-valued world we resent being asked how much money we earn or how much we spend for certain items. Asians don't seem to be inhibited along those lines, much to the embarrassment of Westerners, whose answers make them seem so ridiculously rich!

In our youth-oriented society it is impolite to ask anyone's age, especially that of a woman. In China, where age is treated with respect, who would want to conceal the number of years with their accumulated wisdom? It is, in fact, sometimes difficult for an American to accept gracefully the special consideration accorded gray hair; maybe we don't want to be made to feel old!

The names you can call people without arousing their wrath also vary with the culture. In China we learned that one of the most insulting things you can do is call someone a dog. Creighton Lacy in his little book on a return visit to China, the land of his childhood and young adult years, tells how he inadvertently referred to his tour guide as the "sheep dog of the party" because he so patiently and conscientiously watched over them and kept them from straying. Too late Lacy recalled the offensiveness of such terminology, and it took a good bit of explaining to return to the good graces of the guide. We had a similar experience in Chengdu when one of our students playfully called a staff person the watchdog of our residence hall. We had to explain and apologize not only to her but to the higher authorities of the department.

These episodes help us to understand the implications of the cold-war epithet used against the United States, "the running dogs of foreign imperialism." It also makes us aware of how abusive some Western language has been, perhaps unintentionally. We have all heard the story of the colonial arrogance demonstrated in the Shanghai park which was reserved for use by white residents with a sign declaring that no dogs or Chinese were allowed. To the Chinese the implication was that they were in the same category as dogs. Lacy, who was residing in Shanghai at that time, admits that there were, indeed, signs which prohibited both Chinese and dogs from entering the park, but he says the two were not so blatantly placed side by side as alleged (*Coming Home to China*, 1978). Unfortunately, the fact that they were both on the same sign was serious enough that the resentment has been nursed through these many decades. However, the atmosphere today is much warmer toward foreigners of all nationalities (except Russian, of course) and especially toward their new American friends.

At Home in the Middle Kingdom

During our stay in Chengdu, capital city of the ancient kingdom of Shu, people often told us of the old saying that it is harder to get to Chengdu than to get to heaven. The saying comes from an eighth-century poem entitled "The Road to Shu Is Hard." The poet, who had made the trip over the rugged mountains into the Sichuan basin, describes the obstacles—torrential rivers, wild animals, breathtaking cliffsides "where one can touch the stars." Having reached Chengdu (known as the Brocade City) after surviving all the dangers of the trail, he concluded:

> The Brocade City might be a place for pleasure,
> But it's far better to hurry home.
> The road to Shu is hard, harder than climbing to the Heavens.

Nowadays it is not so hard physically, nor did we find it hard emotionally. We did not share the view that it was better to hurry home!

3
A Long Look Back

Modern Chinese impress me as self-confident, competent individuals, who are aware of their identity and take pride in their ethnic background. But their words often belie that impression of confidence and pride in their roots. There seems to be a tendency to self-depreciation. I think this disparagement of their own achievements and worth is a matter of Chinese courtesy rather than inner conviction. I have experienced the same tendency among overseas Chinese in other Asian countries. My prize example is the occasion of being a guest in an Indochinese home, where we were to partake of an abundant and tasty feast. Our host, as is customary, made the usual speech of warm welcome and apology for the poor hospitality they were about to offer, saying in effect, "The food is very poor; my wife cooked it herself and she is not a good cook." His charming wife sat beside him smiling cheerfully! My American housewife mentality would not allow me to believe he really meant it, or she could not possibly react so benignly!

Likewise, on our China visit we found our college-official hosts frequently apologizing for the poor accommodations they were able to provide in contrast to what we were undoubtedly accustomed at home. I always had to suppress the urge to say, "If we had wanted exactly what we have at home, we should have stayed at home." But it is typical Chinese courtesy to offer the best possible to foreign guests. And I suspect it is also typically Chinese to depreciate their own accomplishments.

A Glorious Past

A closer look reveals the deep pride the Chinese take in the improvements which have been made by their socialist society during the past 30 years. One also finds numerous indications of their positive identification with a long history of past glories in the fields of science and technology, literature, art, language, and philosophy. Even while they proclaim themselves a backward nation, economically poor, uneducated in modern science, and inexpert industrially—a developing nation—one has the feeling that they know it was not always thus and have the assurance it will not always be so.

Signs of past glories are much in evidence in the many restored pagodas, memorial parks, museums, and carefully preserved historic sites—in their ancient treasures of art and literature. To understand the perspective of today's China, we need to take a quick look back at her long history with some of the early claims to world leadership. It may be surprising to some Westerners to learn of the impressive catalog of inventions for which the Chinese are generally given credit. Citing their many mechanical, astronomical, and mathematical discoveries and inventions could fill an entire page. A few of the more common ones will illustrate Chinese ingenuity and the valuable contributions they have made to humankind.

They have given us silk, paper, sundials and clocks, the compass, seismograph, gunpowder, the abacus, wheelbarrow, hydraulic engine, movable-type printing, watertight compartments for ships, and the paddle wheel boat. They recorded solar and lunar eclipses back in the 12th and 14th centuries before Christ and observed Halley's comet in 28 BC (16 centuries before Galileo). They calculated the solar year at 365¼ days in the fifth century BC. Remember pi equals 3.1416 from your school days? Chinese mathematicians had figured it precisely (3.1415927) back in the fifth century BC. Such practical things as canal locks, irrigation and flood control measures, crop rotation and terracing were in use in China long before the Christian era.

Let us now take a quick look at the long and complex history of the peoples who showed such evidence of unusual creativity and scientific vigor. I need not remind you that at best such an overview must be extremely simplified, even simplistic, and incomplete. In tracing the general course of Chinese history, I make no attempt at a balanced coverage of its complexities. While I will follow a somewhat chronological pattern, I will arbitrarily pick out those events and developments which will be of most interest to the average reader, which will shed some light on the things we have traditionally associated with Chinese culture, or which are somehow relevant to our visit and observations. If this brief glimpse arouses your curiosity, you can find many weighty tomes on China's rich and colorful past in which to dig more deeply.

From Prehistoric Legend to Dynastic Reality

Native Americans can take a longer view, but for most of us whose ancestors were the European settlers of the so-called New World, our backward look rarely goes beyond those 17th-century migration dates. Our country only recently celebrated its 200th anniversary. The Chinese look back 2,000 years to their first unified state. The discovery of

Peking man in 1929, along with other fossils, led archaeologists to believe that China might have been inhabited a half million years ago. There is credible evidence of communities existing in China five or six thousand years ago. How would you like to be a schoolchild with a history text covering that time span?

Chinese historians divide time according to dynastic rulers. A dynasty is the succession of rulers from the same genealogical line or family; it may vary in length from a few years to hundreds of years depending upon the family line's ability to supply competent monarchs, and the condition of the empire or fortunes of war at any given time. A ruler was thought to have a "mandate from heaven" to rule over his subjects, whether he had ascended to the throne by inheritance, by murdering a kinsman, or by successful revolt against a former ruler. If the monarch became corrupt, despotic or incompetent, it meant the gods were no longer smiling on him. Even famines, earthquakes, or adverse climate conditions could indicate that he was no longer in heaven's favor. Then the mandate to rule was withdrawn; the people or a powerful competitor could remove him from the throne, and the mandate was bestowed on the new ruler. While this "heavenly" connection allowed him to function as "son of heaven," the ruler was not considered divine, and heaven was on his side only so long as he ruled well and for the good of his people. The right of the subjects to revolt against unjust rulers was established early in Chinese history, and we find it used repeatedly down through the ages.

Our objective here is to gain a nodding acquaintance with a few dynasties to give us a feel for the movement of history and the evolution of the traditions which characterized old imperial China. In referring to names of dynasties I use the modern romanized spelling, which may not agree with that of older books. Where it seems useful for clarity, I'll give the older form in parentheses.

The prehistoric period is veiled in myths, folktales, and legends. There are heroic tales about the famous Yellow Emperor, Huangdi, who was supposed to have ruled about the 26th century BC in the Yellow River area of northern China, where there may have already been a well-organized society with a written language of primitive pictographs, the forerunners of the Chinese characters still in use today. The emperor's wife is credited with introducing the growing of silkworms for making silk cloth. The Xia dynasty (2000-1500 BC) is sometimes named as the first dynasty; also in the Yellow River area, it ruled a society already settled down to an agricultural life. But there is some question whether that dynasty is based on historical fact or folk fantasy.

The Shang dynasty (1500-1000 BC) is considered the first fully authenticated ancient dynasty. Archaeological discoveries of the 20th century have confirmed the earlier folk accounts of a quite advanced civilization. China had emerged from the shadows of myth and legend to an historic entity. Already a form of ancestor worship had developed, as well as the worship of heaven and various gods and spirits. Even at that time there was a huge gulf between the rich and the poor—the aristocrats and the kings building great palaces while the poor lived in pits, caves, or little thatched huts.

Beginnings of Feudalism

In the following centuries the Zhou (Chou) dynasty (11th century BC-221 BC) was the longest reigning dynasty in Chinese history. However, it was broken up into various regional groupings and time periods with no unified rule. The only continuity was that a Zhou ruler was in power in one of the areas during those eight centuries. Feudalism and Confucianism, major influences in China's development, had their beginnings in this era. A lack of strong kings or central government encouraged the rise of feudalism. Nobles built up their own little fiefdoms with peasants cultivating the land for them, subject to them and dependent upon them. They, in turn, paid tribute and taxes to the king.

Agriculture was still the major occupation, but artisans, traders, and soldiers were becoming important segments of the society. Warfare was a favorite pursuit of the aristocratic class, and weapons were developed—including spears, the crossbow, chariots, and leather armor. Horseback riding was introduced, probably from central Asia, allowing for greater speed and mobility in warfare. The Great Wall of China, built to keep out or at least deter potential invaders from the north, was started in 500 BC although it is usually dated from the second century BC, when it was completed and improved. Some historians think that by the end of the Zhou period the Chinese were probably the most numerous people in the world of that time, just as they are today.

The great philosopher Confucius was born around 479 BC. He attracted many disciples, who carried on his doctrines establishing codes of behavior for every layer of society. His writings and teachings became the basis for government, education, and cultural policies and set the moral and ethical tone for personal conduct, family life, and public practice for the next 24 centuries. Even today, after 30 years of communist rule, the traditional Confucian teachings still influence the lives of millions of Chinese, although they have long been suppressed as counterrevolutionary and reactionary.

During the Zhou dynasty we have the growing concept of the Chinese states constituting the Middle Kingdom (Zhong

Guo), a feeling that they were at the center of the world, somehow unique and superior to the surrounding "barbarians"—a term they continued to use for foreigners into the 20th century. (At that time their language had no other term for foreigner.) The middle kingdom concept seems to indicate a growing sense of ethnicity and peoplehood in those times. The Chinese name for China today is still Zhong Guo, the Middle Kingdom.

A United Empire 2,200 Years Ago

The Qin (Chin) dynasty (221-206 BC) ushered in a new phase of China's history, the imperial pattern which was to continue until modern times. The Qin is the shortest of all dynasties, only 15 years in power, but it is of great importance today because it marked the unification of China, the formation of an empire in which all the various feudal and princely states were under the control of one sovereign. Our history lecturer in Chengdu observed that the consolidation of the United States took only 200 years, but the consolidation of China took several thousand years.

Qin Shi Huang was the first, and virtually the last, of this dynastic line. Along with the clan name, Qin, he took the name Shi Huang, which means "first emperor." He evidently was intent on making a clean sweep of the past and beginning a new imperial structure appropriate to the enlarged coalition of states comprising his domain. Qin kings had been ruling in parts of China for at least five centuries, gradually expanding their holdings until by 221 BC they had conquered all of China as it then existed. Qin Shi Huang had become heir to the throne in 246 BC at the age of 12. After he began to rule at age 21, it took him 16 years to consolidate his realm before he declared himself emperor of the entire unified kingdom.

He was a strong administrator, centralizing and standardizing control of the areas within his empire. Modern Chinese emphasize this accomplishment and downplay the extreme cruelty by which this was achieved. He has generally been depicted as merciless in his treatment of conquered external foes as well as in his tactics to quell dissidents within his own realm. Early historians tell us that he ordered the burning of history and philosophy books and the killing of hundreds of Confucian scholars, many by burying alive, in order to maintain thought-control of his subjects.

He divided the area into geographic units and created a bureaucracy for their administration—a practice which was to become a hallmark of Chinese governments for centuries to come. He also standardized the written language, currency, weights and measures; built roads and canals; repaired and added to the Great Wall; and stringently controlled the economic and political life of the people.

Although Qin Shi Huang died in 210 BC after only a brief reign, he had set the pattern for imperial rule which was followed until the establishment of the Republic in 1912. Due to the perfidy of his adviser, one of his sons committed suicide and another was murdered, as was the adviser who was conniving for the throne. This brought an end to the Qin line, but the concept of a unified Chinese people under a central government had been planted, creating the political entity which came to be known as China.

Today, more than 2,000 years later, Qin Shi Huang is much in the news as his extensive and elaborate burial place is being excavated near modern Xian (Sian) [see "China's Incredible Find," *National Geographic*, April 1978]. The life-size army of 6,000 pottery men and horses among the finds thus far seems to indicate that Qin Shi Huang didn't believe the saying, "You can't take it with you." Kings in those days started early and lavished great attention on their tombs, which they hoped would reflect their earthly glory. We are told that some 700,000 conscripts worked 36 years to prepare Qin's final resting-place—a palatial residence fitted with every precious luxury, guarded by an elite honor guard. The countenances of the pottery men are so lifelike that they are believed to have been modeled after the real men of his bodyguard. If surprised by the ego of this emperor, we must remind ourselves that rulers of that age often took with them to their graves the real men, not just clay figures! In fact, we are told that when the bearers of the emperor's body finally placed it in the tomb following great pomp and ceremony, the new emperor—the corrupt son of Qin Shi Huang—ordered the great door to be sealed, thus entombing them as

A pagoda in Shenyang, typical of traditional Chinese architecture.

well. Since they were the only ones who knew the intricacies of the labyrinthine burial site, it was safe from grave robbers.

It is usually assumed that the country of China derived its name from "Chin" (the old spelling of Qin), but our history lecturer questioned this assumption. The Chinese name for China is Zhong Guo, which—as we have noted—means "Middle Kingdom." The foreign version, of course, may have come from "Chin." In any case, the Qin are given credit for creating the China that the world has known for more than 2,000 years. The current regime is polishing up the image of Qin Shi Huang in order to reflect favorably the imperative of a unified China today.

Confucius and the Hans

The Han dynasty (206 BC-220 AD), which followed the founding Qin, ruled for the next four centuries over an empire flourishing in the arts and sciences. Han emperors, who are described as shrewd and pragmatic, continued to consolidate the empire. Significant aspects of their reign were the refinement of the bureaucratic system, acceptance of Confucianism as the state doctrine, and the institution of the examination system for civil-service positions. These scholar-bureaucrats, steeped in Confucian classics, became the elite mandarin class, a prominent part of traditional Chinese life and government.

Confucian moral teachings prescribed the behavior of all from the peasant to the emperor. They became an agent for cultural uniformity. The emperor was to rule by virtuous example and for the good of all the people. He, as "son of heaven," was to be completely obedient to heaven, just as subjects were to be obedient to the ruler, wives to husbands, and children to parents. The doctrine made for a stable society and family if not for innovation or individuality. A university was founded to propagate these teachings, and there was a resurgence of research by historians and scholars to recover the ancient texts, write commentaries, and organize documentary materials. There was an element of religious devotion in the attention given to the study of this philosophy.

The Han period was an age of expansion. In 111 BC northern Vietnam was brought under China's control, to continue there for 1,000 years. A little later Manchuria and Korea became satellites. Ancient records show that in the second century AD the king of Java sent tribute to China's emperor and that an emissary from the Roman emperor Marcus Aurelius paid a visit. Trade with other countries was carried on by land and sea routes, among them the famous

The entrance to the famous Forbidden City in Beijing.

Silk Route, which had long been used to transport silk to central Asia and Persia. Many countries were keen on Chinese silks, but the Chinese had less interest in foreign imports because they had everything they needed at home.

In the Western world the Roman Empire was at its zenith during the Han dynasty. In the Middle East the Christian church had its birth and began to spread. There was much struggle and confusion during this period, but there was also a time of peace and prosperity for China's 60 million people. Aside from maintaining some degree of political and cultural unity, there appears to have been a growth of ethnic unity, as it was at this point that the majority ethnic group began to designate themselves as Hans. As noted before, in today's China about 94 percent of the population is made up of Han Chinese, the rest being small minority groups of more recent addition.

The Dark Ages

The Hans' final years were plagued by peasant rebellions, warlord uprisings, and the declining competence of the emperor—all harbingers of the withdrawal of the mandate to rule. No sovereign proved capable of taking over for a period of 3½ centuries, a time to which some historians refer as the "dark ages" of China. The period from 220 to 589 AD saw a profusion of diverse kingdoms and would-be rulers who competed for heaven's blessings and a piece of the old empire. The territory was first carved up into three kingdoms ruled by three former Han generals—the kingdoms of Wei, Shu, and Wu. The Three Kingdoms period was later romanticized by such literary works as the famous novel *The Romance of the Three Kingdoms,* written 1,000 years later and still being read today. The Shu kingdom has special interest for residents of Chengdu. The ancient kingdom which the poet Li Po found so inaccessible in the eighth century ("The Road to Shu Is Hard") was located in what is now Sichuan (Szechwan) Province and ruled from Chengdu as its capital city. Like modern Sichuan it was in a basin surrounded by mountains. In 1980 we crossed over those mountains, the poet's terrifying obstacle, in just 36 hours by train under very comfortable circumstances.

One outstanding development during the so-called dark ages was the popular acceptance of Buddhism and its growth as a major religion. It had been introduced into China from India as early as 170 AD but had not been immediately accepted. Indian pilgrims traveling to China translated some of the texts into Chinese; Chinese adherents also traveled to India to study the religion and bring back translations of Buddhist writings. Various figures of Buddha found in China indicate that the faith became quite widespread. The period from the fourth to the ninth century is known as the Age of Buddhism in China; the doctrine seems to have attracted a large following, threatening to become the state religion. Confucian scholars, of course, were opposed to it and discounted it as a foreign import. However, in a modified form it exerted substantial influence and has left its mark on Chinese society. Today it remains one of the major religions.

The Sui dynasty (589-618) ruled during a period of general unrest although a number of ambitious projects were undertaken by all-powerful emperors who sometimes used their vast reservoir of human resources as if there were an inexhaustible supply. They extended the Great Wall. A system of canals linked north and south from the Yellow River to the Yangtze. This waterway network proved to be of great future benefit but was built at terrific cost in lives and misery. Historians tell us that in the course of one ten-day period in 607 a million men were put to work on the wall, half of whom died or disappeared (Milton W. Meyer, *China: An Introduction*, p. 117). It is estimated that 5½ million people worked on the waterway projects. In some areas all the common people (presumably men) between the ages of 15 and 55 were impressed into the labor force, and those who could not, or would not, fulfill the demands of the overseers were severely punished. Every fifth family along the route was required to supply one person (child, older man, or woman) to prepare food for the workers. Approximately two million lives were expended on this project. Such was the price in human suffering for this improvement in the trade and communication of future generations. All

A mythical lion guards one of the many ancient buildings.

this probably added to the unrest, and the last Sui emperor was killed by a rebel.

When the Tang dynasty (618-907) took power, the empire had a population of about 130 million. The capital city of Chang-an with nearly two million people is thought to have been the largest city in the world at that time. Chang-an was located on the site of the modern city of Xian, near which the current excavations of Qin Shi Huang's tomb are in process.

Tang Dynasty Accepts Foreigners

In the first part of the Tang era there was considerable expansion of territory as well as in trade and cultural affairs—a time when China was most open to international interaction. Many foreigners were in the capital, and the Chinese traveled far afield to other countries; there was a new openness and tolerance for foreign ideas, literature, and philosophies. Aside from the more mundane trade motive, interest in Buddhism added impetus to foreign contacts. Its popularity shows up in painting, sculpture, and architecture. In spite of the surge of Buddhism, there were several other religions vying for attention. Christianity was first brought to China in the seventh century by the Nestorians. Although they were considered heretics by the Roman Church, they had made converts in the Middle East, central Asia, and India. In Marco Polo's account of his travels in the 13th century, he makes many references to Nestorian Christians. In fact, it is said that the mother of Khubilai Khan was of this religion. In the eighth century, Islam was introduced into China and flourished in certain areas; it still remains strong in modern China among some minority groups.

As a whole, this was a productive period for the literary arts, a golden era for poetry. Some of China's most famous poets—such as Li Po, Du Fu, and Li Bai—lived in the eighth century. Block printing contributed to the literary efforts, the world's first newspaper was printed, and a book printed in 868 is still in existence.

The Making of a Mandarin

Of major interest during the Sung dynasty (960-1279) is the perfection of the examination system and the emergence of the mandarins as a ruling class. Scientific knowledge produced many advances in medicine, pharmacy, mathematics, astronomy, and botany. Achievements in these areas were superior to any in Europe prior to the 16th century. Advanced technology was also being applied to military weapons. Numerous border conflicts were the testing grounds for new weapons.

The examination system for scholar-gentry, who received government appointments on the merit of their academic performance, had been employed for hundreds of years, but it was not until 1065 that it was standardized and administered at regular three-year intervals. While the examination was supposed to cover such areas as history, economics, law, and the sciences, the greatest emphasis was on the literary classics by the Confucian philosophers of the sixth to fourth centuries BC. These exams for candidates who aspired to be civil servants were given at three different levels. At the first step, on the county level, only up to ten percent of the candidates passed. They proceeded to the second rung of the ladder, where again about ten percent passed the exams given in the capital city. The final round was the palace examination, which weeded out still more and determined the rank of the finalists. Examinees were carefully isolated in individual cells for several days during testing. Years were devoted to the preparation and study, to memorizing the Confucian texts, which essentially limited the competition to families wealthy enough to subsidize the scholars. It was common to spend ten years in study, and most received their top degree at about age 35. Fairbank notes that this would be comparable to receiving tenure on an American faculty today (*The United States and China*, p. 44).

We know these scholar-administrators as mandarins, a term which conjures up the image of an intellectual academic in long silken gown, pigtailed hair, hat showing status, and extremely long fingernails testifying to the fact that he could do no manual labor. His was a figure lending itself well to caricature. The stereotyped mandarin is often a character in the traditional opera or drama. In the new China, of course, he is not an acceptable role model since he failed to combine book learning with practical work and his motivation was self-aggrandizement rather than social uplift.

A humorous account of the examination process is given in a book by an expatriate author, who reminisces about his childhood in China. He writes fondly about his second oldest great-uncle who decided to follow an official career, spent his whole life trying to pass the first-level examination, and at age 62 had not succeeded (Chiang Yee, *A Chinese Childhood*). His well-to-do, traditional extended family was able to humor him in this lifetime pursuit. His, of course, was a rather extreme example; most candidates likely gave up after the first few tries and settled for some less prestigious work.

While the government through this practice sought the most talented (according to their rigid prescription and limited definition of academic excellence) for appointment to high position, many posts were filled by other means, including purchase of office, nepotism, and repayment of political favors. But the transcendence of this system did bring about the displacement of the nobility as the ruling class by the scholar-gentry bureaucracy.

Reformer Before His Time

An interesting story from the Sung period tells of a potential great reformer of the bureaucratic system. An 11th-century imperial minister, Wang An-shih, initiated reforms which were well ahead of his time—perhaps too far ahead, as they met with great opposition. He reformed the treasury, introducing a state budget which reduced embezzlement and required fiscal responsibility by government—measures so effective that they are purported to have saved up to 40 percent of national funds. He inaugurated a system of warehouses to store the grain paid to the government as taxes, rather than transporting it to the capital city. This grain was then sold in the collection area and taxes transmitted in cash. He devised a plan for government loans to farmers at low interest rates. Luxury goods and hoarding were heavily taxed. Peasants could make money payments in place of the forced labor, which had always assured a supply of slave labor for government projects.

The populace was organized into ten-family units for local administration and compulsory military service quotas. All members of the unit were held responsible for the misdeeds of any one member. Perhaps this policy was the forerunner of the neighborhood political groups of current communist organizational patterns, with their similar duties of mutual responsibility. It seems the peasants of that day were definitely opposed to the idea.

While the peasants supported the other reforms, the gentry (scholar-administrator class) were loath to lose their forced labor resource; the state officials were not happy to give up the customary practice of supplementing their incomes with a little embezzlement of public coffers, nor did they relish strict account-keeping and budgeting. So Wang An-shih met defeat in his brilliant reform ideas at the time; but he succeeded in shaking up the establishment, and some of his "radical" ideas did find acceptance in later times. What the series of revolutions nine centuries later hoped to accomplish might have been attained by Wang had the people been more cooperative.

One final note: it was during the Sung era, probably in the 11th or 12th century, that the rich, seeking luxurious amusements and pleasurable experiences, introduced the custom of foot-binding. For some strange reason it was considered to have erotic connotations. "Lily feet" became a romantic literary expression. The more practical effect was that the upper classes imposed upon their women this custom which confined them to a childhood of suffering and an adulthood of restricted activity for the next nine centuries. They were not to be freed from it until the nationalist revolutions and women's liberation movements of the 20th century.

The Closed Door

By the end of the 13th century China had acquired the unique characteristics—socially, politically, and culturally—which most Westerners associate with traditional China. The following few centuries proved to be relatively stable and peaceful in spite of an extended reign by "foreign" emperors. But there is the general impression of isolation from the rest of the world; and the "closed door" apparently heightened the "inscrutable Oriental" image, making China the object of much interest and curiosity to the outside world. It is evident that after the 13th century the inventive

The Temple of Heaven, one of the tourist attractions in Beijing.

genius which had produced so many "firsts" far in advance of European nations seemed to have dried up.

John King Fairbank, noted China historian, explains this lag as the result of Confucianism with its focus on human society and personal relationships rather than on man's conquest of nature. This deference to nature shows up in traditional Chinese paintings in which tiny human figures are overshadowed by the dominant nature scene. The Confucian weakness in logic and reasoning, the emphasis on rote memory, the restrictions of Chinese characters in language expression, and the elimination of manual labor from the experience of the scholar are all aspects of this philosophy. The fact that there was no respectable place for manual work in the life of the scholar resulted in a "separation of hand and brain" in contrast to the European pattern which effectively joined the two in developing an industrial society. The very lack of a huge body of written materials such as that to which Chinese scholars had access by virtue of earlier discoveries, may have been an advantage to European scientists and inventors. They were forced to put greater emphasis on reasoning ability over conventional research and memory.

In other words, the falling behind of Chinese inventiveness may have been due more to social circumstances of the time than to any loss of native ability. With the socialist downgrading of Confucian and traditional thought, the Marxist emphasis on self-reliance and rationalism, and the current thirst for modern scientific methods, perhaps the climate is right for a resurgence of the old creative genius.

4

Whatever Happened to the Middle Kingdom?

Our memories tend to retain the most flamboyant images from past exposure to such things as world history. So it is that from our school days we recall the daring exploits of the Mongol "hordes" led by Genghis Khan, those fearsome troops known as the "yellow peril," swooping down from the north in the 13th-century conquest of a vast empire which in time would include all of China. Genghis Khan captured Beijing in 1215, but he was never able to overcome the resistance of the South. It was his grandson, the great Khubilai Khan, who finally defeated the last Sung emperor and established the Yuan dynasty (1279-1368), bringing the Chinese empire under the rule of despised "barbarians" for almost a century.

The Mongols and Other Foreigners

The Mongol rulers of this far-flung realm did not trust placing Chinese in high positions, so they did away with the civil-service exam system and chose Chinese or foreigners only for posts which they could not fill with Mongols. They used foreign mercenaries to augment their military forces and recruited able administrators from many nationalities to help govern this formidable new addition to their empire. The Italian Marco Polo became one of these foreign officials.

He was only 17 years old when he, with his father and uncle, started for China in 1271. He served the Mongols for 17 years as a court official, and when he returned to Italy he carried with him much wealth and a fabulous account of his adventures in China, which gave Europeans their first detailed description of the great exotic empire of the East.

The wide extent of the Mongol domain facilitated the ease and safety of travel. This promoted international relations and brought a rush of foreign visitors desiring to trade in luxury goods, to Christianize the huge populace, to make political and military alliances, or for pure adventure and discovery. The Catholic Church sent its first emissary in 1245, but it was not until 1307 that an Italian Franciscan established a mission in Beijing, who had gathered 30,000 converts by the time of his death in 1352. This early church, like the earlier Nestorians, did not survive after the collapse

Shanghai harbor, reminiscent of Western dominance in China.

of the Mongol empire. The records indicate that many other Christian and Muslim groups were welcomed by the Mongols, but none of them established any lasting roots.

Eventually the foreign dynasty declined and ended with no real change in China's traditional way of life. The Yuan rulers had tried to accommodate to Chinese ways and bridge the gulf between Mongol and Han Chinese cultural patterns. In the end their efforts at acculturation, combined with the overwhelming majority of the Han and the problems of communication over the vast distances, seemed to result in the loss of their own distinctive identity and their assimilation by Chinese culture. Weak successors of Khubilai Khan and the usual peasant rebellions marked the end of foreign rule until the advent of the Manchus three centuries later.

Beginnings of "Foreign Invasion"

The Ming dynasty (1368-1644) is perhaps the most familiar to us in the West because of its famous blue and white pottery, the architectural wonders of the Forbidden City (forbidden to the common people) within the imperial city of Beijing, the exquisite temples and pagodas, the magnificent tombs of the Ming emperors, the Great Wall in its present imposing proportions—all intriguing tourist attractions in the modern world.

After the century of foreign rule the Ming reverted to things "native" Chinese, refining and re-establishing the traditional elements of imperial China: a bureaucracy administered by the scholar-gentry class based on Confucian principles and the civil-service merit system, with Buddhism as the favored religion; a foreign policy built on the tribute system, a diplomacy of pacification through exchange of gifts and the acknowledgment of China as the Middle

Kingdom around which revolved all lesser kingdoms. With this concept of the emperor as the head of the universal political order, he could require all "vassal" kings to pay tribute in the form of gifts and to pay homage by the performance of the kow tow (a series of kneelings and prostrations, touching the forehead to the ground) upon approaching the emperor. This is a Chinese term which we have adopted into the English language, and most of us don't like to kowtow to anyone!

In spite of the turn back to things Chinese, there was a flurry of expeditions and explorations of new sea routes resulting in international exchanges and acceptance of foreign "imports." Among these were some which came either directly or indirectly from the Americas, notably maize (corn), sweet potatoes, peanuts, and tobacco. The Ming tried unsuccessfully to prohibit the cultivation and use of the last. (Did they already know it is injurious to health?) Cotton, imported from south Asia, became one of China's major crops, as it still is today.

It is important to take notice of the trickle of foreign traders and missionaries, with their accompanying gunboats and government safeguards, which became a tidal wave of foreign "invasion" in the centuries to follow. The following Western countries made their entry: the Portuguese in 1514 (gaining a foothold in Macao in 1557), the Spanish by way of the Philippines, the Russians in 1567 and in 1619, the Dutch in 1622, and the British in 1635. (You will recall that at about this time our European ancestors were busy making their way to the New World formerly occupid by the American Indians.)

One of the few success stories of the foreign incursion was that of Matteo Ricci, an Italian student of mathematics and astronomy, a Jesuit missionary under Portuguese sponsorship, who arrived in Macao in 1582. By diplomatic combination of Confucian scholarship, accommodation to the Chinese cultural and religious habits, adoption of the Chinese language and dress, and brilliant expertise in many scientific fields, Ricci over 20 years worked his way up to the imperial court in Beijing, where he was permitted to preach and serve the emperor until his death in 1610. As an example of his sensitive approach, he reportedly prepared a map of the world with China placed diplomatically in the center.

The powerful Ming went the way of all dynastic lines—with weak rulers, grasping courtiers, and greedy royal family members amassing huge estates at the expense of the landless peasants. At its demise China again came under the control of non-Han "barbarians." A general needing help against a rival made an alliance with Manchurian forces. The enemy was subdued; the ally, however, refused to leave and proceeded to take over China for the Manchus.

Resistance to Western Imperialism

The Qing (Ching) dynasty (1644-1911), the name given to the line of Manchu rulers, took control of all China as had the Mongols in the earlier time of foreign domination, but they survived a good bit longer, probably because they adopted more of the traditional patterns of government. They adapted themselves to Chinese life and culture, but they took precautions to maintain their own identity by banning intermarriage and certain customs such as foot-binding. They conscientiously followed the Confucian doctrines which validated their mandate to rule even though they were not ethnic Chinese. To utilize the energies of the scholars which the examination system was still producing, the Qing promoted great literary and artistic projects. The result was a strategic diversion of talent from civic administration, and an agreeable division of labor and prestige.

This final dynasty was in power during what is sometimes called the "Western invasion" of China in the 18th and 19th centuries. We have seen that many Europeans were eager to enter this new potential field for commerce and mission work already in the 15th to 17th centuries but were without much success. The 18th-century Enlightenment period in Europe intensified the interest in Chinese philosophies and religions. Colonial expansion into Asia and the New World, and the pseudo empires of the great European trading companies, continued an avid desire for luxury goods; and the growth of industrial capacity sparked the search for raw materials. In Europe and colonial America household furnishings showed a definite Chinese influence. Such things as Ming porcelain, Chippendale furniture, and Wedgwood china with Chinese patterns were all popular.

But the Middle Kingdom continued to be resistant to the wooing of the West. They had few needs for foreign products, and government policy tended to restrict trade to limited areas mainly in the South. Specific guilds were appointed to handle commercial matters with foreigners; resident aliens were confined to living quarters in designated sections of cities. Western concepts, of course, clashed with Chinese ideas on many issues. The Chinese persistence, for example, in referring to all foreigners as barbarians and the practice of the kow tow did not conform to Western ideas of equality, or even courtesy. Western law emphasized individual rights while the Chinese focused on group responsibility. Foreign traders wanted consistently administered, openly publicized low tariff rates for everyone. And they objected to being required to live in specified areas and to deal only with specified agents in trade negotiations.

The Reality of Power

The British took the lead in bringing pressure to bear; special envoys and emissaries dispatched to Beijing were of little avail in gaining more favorable agreements. Americans, involved with their own affairs and the war for independence, did not enter the China competition until very late in the 18th century. The first merchant ship arrived in 1787. Missionaries began to arrive in the 19th century (first in 1829). This century saw the establishment of the unequal treaties in which Westerners demanded "most favored nation" status in their trade with China, giving equal opportunity to all trading partners. Any concession granted one foreign power could be requested by all, apparently the general practice of the times. While the Americans were critical of British imperialism, they were nonetheless quick to seek their fair share of benefits from the established policies. Like the British, they were not averse to a show of naval power to reinforce their requests.

Open conflict came as a result of the illegal opium traffic, which China was trying to stop. As a result of the confiscation and destruction of a British shipment of opium brought from India in 1839, the first war between China and the West took place. (Were the British remembering the Boston Tea Party?) The British were victorious in this conflict, known as the Opium War, and obtained basically what they had been agitating for in the Treaty of Nanjing, which the Chinese were forced to sign in 1842. This was the first of what came to be known as the "unequal treaties," which regulated foreign trade in China for the next 100 years. The Chinese ceded Hong Kong to the British, paid a $21 million indemnity, awarded trading rights in an additional five ports along with residential concessions, granted a fixed low tariff, allowed foreigners to trade with whomever they wished, and recognized diplomatic equality. (No more kowtowing.)

Several months later another treaty gave foreigners the right of extraterritoriality, another "thorn in the flesh" of the Chinese, which was to last for a century. This meant that foreigners were tried in their own courts according to their own law codes rather than under the legal system of their host country. A similar treaty concluded by Americans in 1844 extended extraterritoriality to civil as well as criminal offenses. The tidal wave of Western invasion had begun, and there was no stopping it. It spelled bad news for the Qing regime, which would hold on for another 60 some years but would see their empire going down the drain, hurried along by the wrenching process and divisiveness of the westernizing influences which were embraced by some Chinese and despised by others.

The Price of Defeat

The empire was torn by many uprisings, partially due to the need for economic and political reforms and possibly also to the impact of the alien intrusion. One of the most severely disrupting was the Taiping Rebellion, led by a peasant who had been converted to Christianity. His plan for the Taiping "heavenly kingdom" was based on some distorted concepts of Christianity, but he did advance some good programs of social reform and land redistribution, which appealed to the oppressed peasants burdened with the ever more exploitive taxes. According to Chinese accounts the movement met with considerable success, sweeping across 17 provinces, capturing 600 cities, and establishing a capital in Nanjing. After holding out from 1851 to 1864, the movement disintegrated for lack of leadership upon the death of the instigator. Western powers cooperated with the imperial government in putting down the revolt.

A memorial on the campus of Beijing University to the American author of many books on China. The inscription reads: "In memory of Edgar Snow, an American friend of the Chinese people, 1905-1972."

The Second Opium War against the British and the French came during the time of this internal struggle. In the settlement of that war in 1856, the Chinese ceded more land, paid new indemnities, and opened up ten more ports plus the Yangtze River to foreign trade. They agreed to open a foreign affairs bureau and permit alien diplomats to live in Beijing; foreigners were allowed to travel in the interior; missionaries received added protection; and the opium trade was legalized. By the third treaty—following further armed clashes with the French, British, Japanese, and Russians (1895-98)—China had been carved into spheres of influence and had consented to further demands, such as railway and mine concessions, investment privileges, and permission to build factories. In general, an imposition of financial and economic imperialism on China had been accomplished.

Over a period of time China's vassal territories had been swallowed up by many of the invading powers. Here is a partial list: Vietnam went to the French; Hong Kong, Kowloon, and New Territories to the British; Macao to the Portuguese; the Pescadores, Taiwan, and part of Manchuria to the Japanese; Kiaochow Bay area to the Germans; some northern ports and railway building rights to the Russians.

The Americans, who had entered the competition rather late, had taken no territory. In order to protect their own rights and apparently out of concern for Chinese rights, they put forward a reformulation of an earlier open-door policy, seeking to freeze the spheres of influence and calling for equal tariff and transportation charges in all spheres. Their efforts to get other foreign powers to agree to these proposals were represented by Americans as an effort to promote justice. To Chinese eyes it looked like a political agreement to carry out the joint partitioning of China.

After the humiliation of the empire by the spate of foreign wars, the dissatisfaction of Chinese seeking reforms, and the conservative stance of the despotic Empress Dowager Cixi, who was in control during the last decades of the century, the time was ripe for another rebellion. The Boxer Rebellion in 1900-01 was led by members of a secret society, but it was supported by many government officials even though it was ostensibly directed against the Qing rulers. In reality it took a very antiforeign turn. Some see it as a reaction against what the Chinese perceived as aggression by foreign imperialists and against the rise of a new class of Christian converts who were protégés of foreign missions under the protection of their governments. This new class of Christian Chinese were, of course, suspected of collaborating with the "foreign devils" (a term used, like "barbarian," for anyone who was not Chinese) who were interfering in China's internal affairs and imposing their alien ideas upon an unwilling host nation. Many Chinese Christians were killed along with missionaries and other foreigners in this sudden outburst of violence. Chinese today picture it as an antiimperialistic, patriotic movement, which was brutally put down by a joint force of eight foreign powers in collaboration with their own unjust imperial rulers.

The Boxer Protocol signed by China in 1901 need not be detailed for our purposes. It was a continuation and extension of the earlier concessions, demands which seemed very harsh to the Chinese. (Of the more than $300 million indemnity exacted by 13 countries, the United States later returned its share to be used for Chinese education.) The Boxer Protocol left China a humiliated, defeated nation in subjection to the foreign powers. In our long look back, space forces us to choose among the myriad of events without adequate investigation of causes, consequences, and underlying currents in the social and economic movement of the times. In this too brief survey we have been trying to see things from the Chinese point of view, to sketch the major confrontations and trends which for the last 80 years has fed the resentment against "imperialist aggression," and to help us understand those feelings.

Revolutions and Republics

Some Chinese had for years felt that the only answer to China's many problems was the complete modernization of their country, the revamping of its government, and the formation of a constitutional democracy. One of the proponents of this theory was Dr. Sun Yat-sen. With the deterioration of the Qing regime and the growing unrest across the empire, the time was ripe for change and Sun was conveniently at hand. He had been active during the 1890's organizing, gathering support, and raising funds both at home and abroad. Known as the father of the nationalist revolutions and still one of China's favorite heroes, Sun Yat-sen led an uprising in Wuhan in October of 1911, which quickly became a national movement with such success that by the end of the year he was elected president of a provisional government with its capital at Nanjing. The Republic of China (ROC) was born.

I digress briefly to show the esteem in which Sun Yat-sen is still held more than 50 years after his death and following more than 30 years of communist rule. We Americans tend to refer to the high-buttoned, four-pocket jacket worn by Mao Zedong and millions of Chinese men and women as Mao jackets. Many times during our Sichuan sojourn we were corrected on that score. It is not a Mao jacket but a Sun Yat-sen jacket; Sun was the one who first popularized it, and the people still honor him by wearing it. I'm not sure whether this would have been said during Mao's heyday, but it could well be that the jacket really does symbolize the nationalist revolutionary spirit inculcated by Dr. Sun and the early advocates of a republic.

Back to the revolution. The formation of the Republic brought to an official end the ancient empire with its long and colorful parade of emperors (for better or for worse) and the basic imperial structures, which had survived for more than two millennia. The next few decades were to require wrenching adjustments in the search for new political forms, new philosophical bases, and practical ways of dealing with continued foreign encroachment, economic distress, and the building of a new Chinese identity. With China we now make the leap from the age of feudalism into the modern world.

The last of the Qing dynasty abdicated the throne in February of 1912, and the general of the imperial army, Yuan Shi-kai, ostensibly joined forces with the revolutionaries;

hopes were high for a new and better form of government after the years of deteriorating empire. Sun Yat-sen envisioned a new China with a democratic form of government, with economic and land reforms to ease the burdens of the poor, with a socio-political system which would strengthen the will of the common people to evict the foreign "invaders" and return control to the Chinese, who would transform the tottering empire into a fully modernized nation. This dream was not to be realized.

Sun Yat-sen was soon pressured to step down from the presidency in favor of Yuan Shi-kai. The general did not have the support or the ability to carry out the necessary reforms and establish a democracy. For all practical purposes the "warlords" took over. These warlords seemed to be leaders of disparate regional groups wishing to protect their own advantages, or military commanders who wished to build their own little empires. Sun Yat-sen organized another revolutionary party, the Kuomintang (National People's Party), and continued his efforts at reform. The Republic was on the allied side in World War I and in the peace parley at Versailles tried unsuccessfully to get the unequal treaties revoked. Actually, it was not until 1943 that the Americans gave up their extraterritorial rights in China, 99 years after having acquired them.

Two Kinds of Nationalists

During World War I, Japan began a series of aggressive acts against China, which—along with the Versailles failure—triggered nationalistic, anti-Japanese movements among students. The most important one was the May 4th Movement (1919) in Beijing; Chinese communists regard it as the beginning of the movement which culminated in the founding of the Chinese Communist Party (CCP) in 1921 with a membership of about 70. Both the CCP and Sun's Kuomintang party accepted Russian aid, and it was through Russian encouragement that they formed the United Front, in which Kuomintang nationalists and Communist nationalists combined forces to work at the task of reunifying China, ridding her of foreign domination, and rebuilding the nation (1924-27). During this time of less than successful teamwork, Sun Yat-sen died (1925); and Chiang Kai-shek, who had been a leading general of the Kuomintang forces, gradually assumed control of the party as well. He was officially confirmed as commander in chief of the Nationalist Army and chairman of the party in 1928, and maintained those positions throughout the wars that were to follow.

The flimsy United Front coalition could not long endure. With Chiang Kai-shek's rise to power and his concentration on bringing the warlords into his camp, the communists were expelled from the Nationalist-controlled government in 1927. Mao Zedong took leadership among the communist contingent, and we have the beginning of the long struggle between the two groups, who were supposedly working for the same ends—a unified, stable, democratic, independent Chinese state—but could not agree on the methods. The battle lines were drawn, with "leftist" nationalists joining Mao and the communists, and "rightist" nationalists joining Chiang and the Kuomintang (KMT).

But it was not to be a neat little civil war between two opposing Chinese teams. Most Western nations were concerned with Japan's growing strength and incursion into its neighbor's territories. The United States felt that world peace and stability, as well as the pursuit of their own self-interests, depended on a strong, unified (and, of course, non-communist) China. Assuming that Chiang Kai-shek and the Kuomintang would be the most likely to ensure this result, the United States placed its bet on his team. American support in the form of troops, supplies, counsel, and money continued to flow to Chiang Kai-shek through all the wars of the next two decades and on into the transplanting of his government of the Republic of China on Taiwan.

Chiang established his government headquarters in Nanjing and was accepted by foreign nations as head of the Chinese government. Mao established himself in a mountainous region of south central China, organizing his followers and the local peasants on the model of Russian communist administrative units and proclaiming the first Chinese Soviet Republic of Jiangxi (Kiangsi) in 1931. But during this jockeying for power and the continuing instability of the entire country, Japan took the opportunity to intensify and extend her invasion of China.

Mao's faction declared war on Japan and called for all-out resistance, but Chiang at this point seemed more concerned with rooting out communism and gave priority to his "campaigns of extermination" from 1931 to 1933. His strategies were unable to contain the determined communist forces until in 1934, with the help of Western planning, his troops forced Mao to make the spectacular retreat known as the Long March.

The Long March into Civil War

And, indeed, a long and perilous march it was. With troops and supporters estimated at from 80,000 to 100,000, they made a precipitous exit from Jiangxi on a march that lasted from October 1934 to October 1935. The 6,600-mile trip took them through 11 provinces, across 18 mountain ranges and 24 rivers, over impossible terrain under harassment by Kuomintang armies and attacks by local warlords, and at the mercy of incredible weather conditions. They marched 235 days and 18 nights, averaging 17 miles per day. At the end of the ordeal only about 20,000, including most of the leaders, had survived and reached Shaanxi (Shensi) Province, where a new camp was established at Yanan, which was to be the communist headquarters for the next ten years. A few honored survivors of the Long March are still encountered in China; some are still in important government posts.

During the Long March, Mao was formally elected chairman of the Central Committee, officially marking a leadership which he had already exercised and would continue to hold for more than 40 years. The superhuman feats and heroic deeds of the Red Army and the communist cadres during this remarkable trek have become legendary. The tens of thousands who lost their lives are considered patriotic martyrs; the hardships of the primitive living conditions at Yanan in the early days were something of an endurance test of the faithful. There is no question that Mao was adept at inspiring patriotic fervor and loyalty among his followers. In forming his government at Yanan, as in Jiangxi, he emphasized the role of the peasants as the backbone of the movement. As new areas were "liberated," cadres of workers and activities were organized as propaganda teams, land reforms were carried out, education and literacy were promoted, and the crippling practice of foot-binding was eliminated—symbolically liberating women and inviting their participation in the revolution.

In his well-known book *Red Star Over China,* Edgar Snow describes his visit to Mao's headquarters. It is a fascinating account of life in the revolutionary enclave behind the lines of the war against the Japanese. His is a sympathetic account, but one well worth reading for an understanding of the ground swell of popular support which

A statue of Mao Zedong, the towering leader who inspired patriotic fervor and deep loyalty among his many followers for 40 years.

eventually put the communists into power in China.

The Japanese were proceeding undeterred with the occupation of their giant neighbor. Mao and some of the warlords were proposing a second united front effort in 1935, but Chiang Kai-shek rejected the idea. His mind was changed by an incident which occurred in December of 1936. Chiang had ordered a Manchurian warlord serving as a general of the Northwest Army to attack the communists in that area. But the warlord general, whose homeland was already overrun by the Japanese, was more concerned about the continued Japanese encroachment. When Chiang came to Xian for a consultation, he was kidnapped by the warlord and forced to agree to a united front approach to stop the Japanese. Zhou Enlai was sent as the negotiator for the communists, and a Second United Front was formed by the three factions. The communists agreed to put their army under Chiang's command, and the warlord pledged the support of his troops. The maneuvers which they went through in order to "save face" for Chiang while forcing him to comply make interesting reading.

Many Chinas and Their Allies

This cooperative effort was shaky at best, but some action was imperative. The Japanese had taken over sizable pieces of territory and even formed a puppet government in Nanjing, forcing Chiang to evacuate his capital to Chongqing. China was now carved up in a new way. Besides this puppet state, Chiang ruled over what was known as Free China, consisting mainly of the western and southwestern provinces. Mao's "liberated areas" were expanding in the Northwest, and the warlords were continuing to operate around the fringes. The foreign settlements (and their home nations) were supporting Chiang's Free China; many of them had moved to the interior to avoid Japanese control. World War II entered the picture to complicate matters still further, distracting the United States from its efforts to make China a big power and diverting some of its resources to the Western front. But the Americans' major effort in the Asian theater was the defeat of the Japanese, with some concern for keeping Russia from becoming an ally of the Chinese communists. They wanted to avoid a destructive civil war in China if at all possible.

Barbara Tuchman's book *Stilwell and the American Experience in China* gives an eye-opening account of these war years as revealed by the papers and diaries of General Joseph Stilwell, who was posted in China to assist Chiang Kai-shek. While American goals in assistance to China were more or less clear, Washington never seemed able to arrive at an effective policy with respect to the practical achievement of those goals. One gets the impression of interdepartmental squabbles (both in the State Department and the armed services) based on personal ambition, patronizing attitudes toward the Chinese, blind allegiance to Chiang's sometimes despotic tendencies, arbitrary decisions dictated by short-term expediency, and failure to see which way the political winds were blowing with respect to the loyalties of the Chinese masses.

Granted that hindsight is better than foresight, one still can't resist asking the question Tuchman raises (*Notes From China*, 1972). What would have been the course of history if Mao had come to Washington in 1945? It is now known that he had requested such talks 4½ years before taking national power, before the devastating civil war, the outcome of which was almost certainly inevitable at that point—the American aid to the loser destined only to prolong the suffering and alienate a large segment of humanity. It is now known that this effort by Mao and Zhou Enlai to establish a working relationship with President Roosevelt did not even receive the courtesy of a response. Twenty-seven years later another president (Richard Nixon) made the much longer trip—emotionally and ideologically—to Beijing to open dialogue with the very same two leaders.

Sources of Power

How can one explain this unpredicted victory of the underdog, who was without modern technology, without the assistance of foreign funds and materials (even communist Russia was backing Chiang Kai-shek during the Japanese War and World War II), without air power, and with three enemy camps on Chinese soil besides the Japanese (the shared enemy)? Toward the end of this period the Republic was being overwhelmed by internal problems, which Chiang could not, or did not, effectively confront. He ruled a restless citizenry weary of war, crippling inflation, and charges of graft and corruption in high places. Chiang himself was holding four major offices at the time but tended to blame all China's ills on his Western allies, their unequal treaties and failure to give enough help to his sometimes unrealistic military plans.

While the Nationalists had a modern army with foreign equipment, it was trained for traditional warfare. When faced with the guerrilla tactics practiced by the communists, they did not have the flexibility to respond. In the face of difficult logistics they reverted to the old imperial practice of living off the land, commandeering food supplies and animals without compensating the peasants. They thus added to the woes of the rural populace rather than offering them an improved situation. Chiang, with his upper-class mentality and life-style, did not inspire the loyalty of the peasants.

In contrast, Mao's forces were trained in guerrilla warfare compatible with the difficult terrain. They developed a territorial base where an adequate food supply could be had, paying the peasants for supplies and offering manpower where needed. They projected the image of defenders of the common people—a basic tenet of Mao's revolutionary theory. He often used the "fish in water" metaphor: the troops are the fish and the people the water; the fish can survive only with the support of the water. Propaganda teams were used to mobilize the support of the local people so that sharing their resources became a patriotic duty and privilege. The key to the communist success appears to be the winning of the hearts and minds of the peasant masses. Chiang's bourgeois following was made up of more influential members, but they were far outnumbered by the poor peasants on whom Mao staked his chances of ultimate victory.

From Hot Wars to Cold War

With the defeat of Japan at the end of World War II, we near the end of another era. Despite American efforts for a united front, a military truce, and a coalition government, China was plunged into civil war. Neither the Republic nor the communist state was willing to give up the advantages they held. Chiang had made some reforms, but they came too little and too late. The three years of bitter struggle was a more intensive continuation of the drive for supremacy, with the communists gradually gaining the upper hand.

While the Nationalist cause was deteriorating in the summer of 1949, the communists were at work organizing their political and administrative structures for a new, socialist China. In his speech inaugurating the People's Republic of China in Beijing on October 1, Mao used that oft-quoted phrase, "The Chinese people have stood up!" Then came the really hard part of a revolution—the day-to-day administering of social and economic justice for millions of real people.

Three months later Chiang Kai-shek, with some two million followers, retreated to Taiwan and established his Republic of China in exile. When the Korean War broke out in 1950, Taiwan assumed great prominence in the American strategy for containing communism in east Asia. The Seventh Fleet was dispatched to Taiwan Strait to prevent a PRC attack on the ROC and to diffuse Chiang's threat to return to "liberate" the mainland. This action—along with military aid and advisers to Taiwan, a 1954 mutual defense treaty, and billions of dollars in aid in the ensuing years—effectively established the two-China political policy, which has complicated international relations ever since and still poses thorny diplomatic problems.

Chiang Kai-shek continued as president of the ROC until his death in 1975, at which time the mantle passed to his son (in true dynastic tradition?). In 1949 the ROC was recognized by half of the United Nations members and named as one of the "big five" on the Security Council. But the question of which China was the real China (as both agreed that there could be only one China) has been a perennial source of dispute. In 1971 the United States responded to friendly overtures by the People's Republic. In the same year, the PRC replaced the ROC in the United Nations, and by 1976 only 27 countries recognized the ROC as spokesman for all of China. The still unresolved relationship of the two Chinas one hopes will be allowed to be settled peaceably by the two parties themselves, without undue interference by other international empire-builders.

In the PRC, Taiwan is still considered a province of

China, and there is much nostalgic talk of her "return to the motherland." So far the issue has kept a low profile, with the PRC declining to use force to regain control while stubbornly resisting the idea of the island as a separate nation. The Nationalists on Taiwan are just as stubbornly insisting that they represent the real China and will never give up their claim to be recognized as such. While they talk loudly, they are quietly carrying on a fairly large volume of trade routed through Hong Kong, to the advantage of both sides. Some experts advocate, and predict, that the solution will be for Taiwan to join the People's Republic as an autonomous region. The pre-1949 Taiwanese, who are a majority in numbers, have little political clout but must be considered in reaching a satisfactory solution.

This problem, along with other unfinished business, we now leave as we take up the latest stage of Chinese nationhood—the experiment in socialism. Refusal to recognize the PRC kept the door closed to Americans for a quarter of a century and created a certain mystique around one-fourth of the world's population; there is now an insatiable curiosity to peek through the opening door in an effort to understand what has transpired there in the intervening years. Is the concept of the middle kingdom still alive in the hearts of today's Chinese? Will they regain the confidence they once felt as the center of the universe and be able to transform a struggling developing nation into a fully modernized world power as they so ardently desire?

The Socialist Pattern for the New China

The new democratic government inaugurated after the Chinese communist military victory was based on the guiding principles of Marxism-Leninism as interpreted by Mao. Large landholdings were to be equitably redistributed among the masses, and the means of production were to be owned by all the people (the state). Ideals set forth were the elimination of all classes; an end to the exploitation of one class or individual by another class or individual; the erasure of distinctions between mental and manual labor, between workers and peasants, between intellectuals and the unlearned, between city dwellers and country dwellers.

The social contributions of all people were to be appreciated. The productivity of all was to be developed to full capacity, allowing each to fully exercise his talents and abilities. All were to share educational and cultural benefits so that all might enjoy a materially and spiritually good life. These admirable objectives were to be achieved through the collective efforts of the Chinese people.

In Mao's writings it is clear that he envisioned a classless society (communism) as the ultimate goal—a society which ensures all human beings equality with respect to social, political, and economic rights and privileges. It is also clear that Chinese leaders have not claimed to have reached that ideal state. In the interim they are committed to building a socialist society in which all have a greater share in political and social decisions, and equal access to the resources available at this point in history. Admittedly, this requires self-sacrifice, self-reliance, frugality, and persistent hard work.

The Communist Party has been in control for 32 years now. They have made outstanding progress; they have made many mistakes. Some people have not been convinced of the pleasures of the socialist demands for self-sacrifice, self-reliance, simple life-style, and just plain hard work. Many of the upper-economic class moved early to Hong Kong or Taiwan to preserve their way of life. But some stayed and willingly or unwillingly threw in their lot with the revolutionaries attempting to revitalize and transform China under the leadership of Mao and Zhou Enlai. The disadvantaged poor and powerless, by far the largest number, found their lives immensely improved. They were still poor, but everyone was poor. At least they had food, clothing, and shelter; and they had found that they were important to the nation—their own feelings of self-worth were enhanced.

The masses found a voice in politics and felt the power of a group which must be considered in setting national policy. There were no longer beggars or starving people in the streets. Communist moral standards were high; Westerners sometimes call them prudish or puritan. Prostitution was abolished, venereal diseases eliminated. Life expectancy increased as health care and diet improved. Millions were enjoying the benefits of literacy for the first time. Workers were assured of the dignity of their labor, however menial. The regimented and controlled life is a seemingly inevitable result of dictatorships, whether of the right or of the left, an individual dictator or a "dictatorship of the massess" as the PRC styles itself. But Chinese were making the decisions affecting Chinese—for good or ill (and some of them were ill, as we shall see).

Since 1977 socialist China has been opening itself once more to outside influences. How are the billion Chinese, so recently released from feudalism and imperial traditions, adjusting to the facts of life of the 1980's? I can't presume to answer that question, but by sharing a few experiences and insights I hope to better acquaint my readers with a basically friendly, intelligent, and aspiring quarter of our world neighbors.

5

Serve the People

To be a good socialist is to be willing to "serve the people"—a phrase which we heard often among the Chinese. Mao Zedong's more than 50 years of leadership of the communist movement and the People's Republic put much emphasis on the working together of the masses of common people to bring about a new day in China. Unity and concern for others was a major element of Mao Zedong Thought, which formed the ethic of the new person and the new society which he envisioned. Several generations have undergone the political and ethical education of Marxism-Leninism-Mao Zedong Thought. Among the current generation of the faithful, the constant admonition to "serve the people" is apparently taken quite seriously.

Oriental Versus Occidental

Before considering the revolutionary life-style demanded by the Chinese communists if they are to be successful in building a new society, we should take a look at basic philisophy, attitudes, and values to be found in old China and note some differences to be expected between Oriental and Occidental peoples. To be sure, I will be generalizing, and clearly we can't fit everyone (of either group) into neat pigeonholes. A major difference seems to be that of individualism versus group orientation. This affects the role of the individual in respect to life's relationships—in family, state, community, occupation, and friendship. It shapes attitudes toward privacy, love, competition, conflict, morality, service, politics, and concepts of freedom.

The distinguishing features of present-day Chinese values are not entirely the results of Marxist political education of

A Buddhist monk, representing a tradition that still affects the culture and thinking of many modern Chinese.

recent decades. They are also rooted in the centuries of Confucianism, Taoism, and traditional religion. These philosophies and religious beliefs had already established a framework which stressed unselfish loyalty to family and friends, unquestioning obedience to society and the state. The Chinese had long been oriented to the individual's duty in the achievement of society's goals rather than personal fulfillment. They tended to view the individual's role to be the finding of the proper niche from which to participate in the objectives of the state and society, taking pride in cultural identity and contributions to the welfare of the whole people. This meant a sublimation of individual desires to the good of the group, be it family, work force, or government. It also meant a different concept of the freedoms which we Westerners so highly prize and frequently use as measuring sticks for the "freedom" of the rest of the world.

The Chinese tend to emphasize group freedoms: freedom to have access to food, clothing, and shelter; freedom to enjoy the benefits of work and the stability of a basic, ordered society. We put more emphasis on individual freedoms: freedom of speech, of movement, of the press, of choice—in job, education, life-style, and economic pursuit. Perhaps this emphasis stems from our background of a favored economic condition which has permitted us the luxury of many options. We are part of a relatively young, pioneering society, which has admired the achievements of the rugged individualists who make it to the top, the self-made individuals who do not look to their contemporaries as support but as competition. We are more *person* oriented than *people* oriented. We are unwilling to give up our concepts of personal freedoms; but we should be aware that our world view differs from that of many of our fellow inhabitants on this planet earth.

Socialist Transformation

With this understanding of some basic differences in point of view, let us consider how the Chinese have responded to the task of nation-building, having accepted Marxism as their guiding principles. The creation of the "new person" and, consequently, the "new society" was the goal of Chinese socialism during the revolution as it has been in the republic which emerged after the communist victory. Political education of the masses of people was designed to strengthen their moral commitment to transforming their own lives and thus build a new nation which would accord a greater degree of dignity, respect, and equality to every person. This required not only a struggle against all the evils of the old system but a continuous struggle against corrupting influences creeping into the new. On the positive side it meant a new life-style. The apparent position was that all people are capable of being transformed through "thought" education and manual work. One lecturer told us that even the capitalist class is now part of "the people;" after 30 years the majority have been transformed into laborers and productive citizens of the new China.

What was this new life-style to be? Basically, it was to be a life of plain living and hard work. It was to be a simple life of self-reliance, frugality, sharing, social discipline, cooperation; it called for a community committed to accomplish change by joint effort. Physical work, honesty, high moral standards, and service were acclaimed instead of personal success, fame, wealth, or position. The people's welfare was to be placed ahead of personal ambition or fulfillment. Put in negative terms (the Chinese seem to love "anti's"), this meant anti-individualism, anti-elitism, anti-careerism, anti-competition, and anti-acquisitiveness.

Transformation of persons was to come about through

political education, through self-criticism, through giving criticism and receiving criticism from others. It meant a change in habits, customs, ways of thinking, and expectations. The highest demand was for sacrificial, humble service to others and to the whole community (the state). Leaders were expected to devote themselves heart and soul to the service of the people. Those who wanted to be leaders were to be the most dedicated servants of all. (That has a New Testament ring.)

Service Is Respected

Through the years the service ideal has been quite successfully inculcated in the lives of many Chinese. Since service is no longer considered demeaning but a measure of patriotism, they need not feel inferior to those whom they serve. I loved those signs in restaurants, air terminals, and hotels that said, "No tipping allowed." Especially where foreigners were involved, it was something of a statement of self-reliance, an independence that would not bow to the indignity of a tip, which smacks of charity. (I hope this analysis is not just a reflection of my own aversion to the tipping system!) The decree that cadre dealing with foreigners should not accept gifts from them reinforced the image of a people trying to stand upright, negotiating from a sense of equality and not being seduced into the corruption and bribery so common to undeveloped countries' dealings with highly developed ones. (I must say, however, that the Chinese are not strictly consistent as they love to give gifts to their guests!)

"Serve the people" is still a dominant theme in the political education, which begins at an early age. For many it becomes equivalent to the biblical injunction to "love your neighbor." With the people geared to group success, it is difficult to conceive of keen competitiveness, violent conflict, a highly romanticized concept of love and marriage, or moral standards which rest on the argument that "what I do is my own affair and no one else's business." Political slogans and campaigns for moral and physical betterment of society are more acceptable to PRC citizens than they would be to Westerners, who consider such persuasion to be propaganda designed to limit personal behavior. Propaganda in China, by the way, denotes publicity without the negative connotation we attach to it.

Children's books, even on the kindergarten level, highlight the joys of cooperation and service in the classroom and at play. College athletics, while played to win if possible, do not seem so fiercely competitive. In one incident, when antagonistic feelings were aroused in a soccer game, team members and coach went through a "criticism" session to try to analyze where they may have been at fault or had in any way contributed to the ill will. Undesirable housing or job assignments are met with much less acrimonious complaint than we would expect.

Lest this all sound so ideal as to be unreal, let me hasten to add that while the service ideal is accepted and mostly dutifully practiced, there are indications of a growing reversion to more individual ambitions as government policies moderate. One can sense a very human concern for the betterment of one's own lot in life and the advancement of one's family fortunes, but not the sharp competition of our own society. With the anticipated advent of modern technology and impersonalization, I suspect that service to the people will be a less important aim for many workers. And as economic conditions improve, there is likely to be less motivation for cooperative effort and mutual help.

We have often wondered whether our college motto—

"Culture for Service" (a turn-of-the-century phrasing, which at times seems a bit "square" to contemporary American youth)—was perhaps instrumental in our being accepted for an exchange program in the new China. Also, our Study-Service Trimester was intriguing to our Chinese hosts, who seemed to feel right at home with such terminology. We were "serving the people" by helping to teach English. Besides the service aspect, the SST program incorporated the practical, which socialist China has made an effort to combine with book learning. Study and work programs were familiar to Chinese educators. Mao is often quoted as having once said, "To know the taste of a pear, you must eat the pear." To understand life you must experience it. To be educated for a task you must perform the task.

What Role for the Schools?

The educational system was to be a major instrument in political, social, and economic change in the new People's Republic. Mao, in his essay "On New Democracy"—published already in 1940—set forth three main qualities for the education program of the future: national, scientific, and popular. These themes were adopted in 1949 for the culture and education program of the PRC. The national theme called not only for the ideological training of the people but for providing the needed skills for rapid economic development. Education was to be scientific or, as Mao liked to say, "seeking truth from facts" in order to eliminate old feudal or superstitious ideas.

The scientific aspect also called for the "unity of theory and practice," combining formal education with its practical application (book learning along with physical labor). The third theme, popular, was to ensure that educational opportunity be made available to the common people

Beijing University, one of the institutions of higher learning trying to make up for time lost during the Cultural Revolution.

Professor Nie teaching the Chinese language to American students.

(peasants and factory workers) as well as to the intellectual elite class fostered by the former imperial system. The new democratic system was to do away with the entrenched privileged, self-perpetuating, urban elite and guarantee that all working people and their children enjoy educational facilities, preparing them for full participation in the new China's development and governance.

In the last half of the 19th century some efforts to reform education were made. The missionary movement was influential in demonstrating Western patterns through the growing network of mission schools. Some Chinese noted Japan's successful borrowing from Western culture and advocated the same for China. By the 1920's there was a shift to U.S. influence when John Dewey, eminent American educator, spent a year lecturing in China and one of his associates was sent to assist in formulating a plan for education under the Nationalist government. In communist areas Mao, who had been a primary teacher himself in his youth, established schools at all levels, giving special attention to vocational training, adult education, and vigorous literacy programs.

These preliberation efforts were under Russian advice and dominance, as were the early years of the PRC. During the 1950's many Soviet specialists were teaching in Chinese universities and giving aid in curriculum and textbook planning, teaching methods, and policymaking. Soviet materials were translated into Chinese, and Russian replaced English as the most popular foreign language. Many Chinese students were sent to study in Russian universities. This, of course, all ended by 1960, when the Chinese and Russians began their present feud.

During the 1950's there had been a phenomenal increase in schools and school attendance. The illiteracy rate, which had been estimated at 85 percent (some say as high as 95 percent in the rural areas), had taken an incredibly rapid drop as a result of the nationwide literacy campaigns. More than 80 percent of the school-age population were in primary schools and a substantial number in secondary schools, in sharp contrast to preliberation figures. Many factories and communes established schools during the Great Leap Forward in 1958-59. Schools were tied closely to productive labor, attempting to coordinate technical studies with the daily task. A student might spend half of his time in the classroom and half at work on a farm or in a factory.

The school system had started with five levels of instruction: (1) preschool (nursery and kindergarten) for ages 3-7, (2) primary school of six years for ages 7-12, (3) middle school of six years (ages 12-17) with special vocational, short-term, or spare-time schools for adults, (4) higher education at colleges, universities, or other institutions, and (5) cadre schools for political and leadership training of people in public office or leadership positions. ("Cadre" covers a broad range of administrators or workers in the government or party.)

A Leap Backward for Education

The Great Leap Forward (discussed in a later chapter), which attempted to carry out Mao's slogan of "walking on two legs" (developing agriculture and industry simultaneously), stressed the union of the theoretical and practical in education. At first it inspired grand new efforts at enlarging and improving education. The withdrawal of Russian experts, the inadequacy of staff for the newly organized schools, and the economic failure of the Great Leap brought about a severe setback in the education system. It forced a reduction of the 12-year school program to a 10-

year system (five primary and five secondary), which is still in effect.

Before the educational system could regain the lost ground, it became engulfed in the "red" versus "expert" controversy (see also chapter 8), which culminated in the Great Proletarian Cultural Revolution, disrupting China's educational hopes for a decade, from 1966 to 1976. This fiasco, which affected the lives of all people in all aspects of China's development, was especially disastrous to education. It was probably triggered by the Socialist Education Movement, which the Chinese Communist Party initiated in 1962 with the intent to "educate the proleteriat" (make intellectuals of the peasants and workers) and to "turn intellectuals into laborers and revolutionaries." To assist in this leveling process large numbers of primary- and secondary-school graduates were sent to the rural areas to help speed up production.

At the same time, there were top government leaders (including Liu Shaoqi, president of the PRC) who felt that industrial development could not wait for the education of all the masses but should focus on training a corps of specialists to manage and expedite the needed technical advancement. This struggle at the top brought about the nationwide struggle known as the Cultural Revolution. In the current rehashing of this period much is heard about the trauma experienced by "intellectuals." While we Americans reserve that term for persons with extraordinary mental capacity (eggheads?), in China the term seems to apply to any person with at least a middle-school (secondary level) education.

As guests of an educational institution at a time when past mistakes were discussed surprisingly quite freely (about the time when the Gang of Four were being tried for crimes of the Cultural Revolution), we got a patchwork picture of some of the unfortunate events of those chaotic years. Realizing the picture is drawn from sources with widely divergent attitudes and experiences, we make no glib general conclusions. Even in the freer, more optimistic atmosphere, there hovers remorse for what might have been, perhaps a sense of risk in the bright future.

For a time during this upheaval virtually all schools were closed down. When they reopened, it was with totally different standards, administration, admissions policies, curriculum, and format—all reflecting the political and revolutionary aims of the ultraleft wing of the struggle. Practical work was re-emphasized. College entrance exams were suspended and preference given to families of peasants and workers; children of the privileged intellectual types were not eligible and were often sent to the countryside to learn the benefits of laboring with the masses. Academic standards were lowered to accommodate the new students who were academically unprepared for "mental" work.

STC and the Stinking Number Nines

Sichuan Teachers' College was closed from 1966 to 1972, as were most all institutions of higher education. Many teachers and the students who were not out rampaging with the Red Guards, were sent to work in the country. Families were often separated; innumerable stories of hardship and tragedy can be told. Almost two generations of college students missed out on their chance at higher education. (Some have been able to regain the lost opportunity; others never will.) Most families engaged in white-collar work—the "intellectuals" who were administrators, doctors, teachers, civil servants—experienced harassment and ill-treatment, sometimes extreme. We were, of course, most closely associated with that group of intellectuals who were "serving the people" as teachers, whose major task was preparing others to serve in that capacity. Our friends told us that during the Cultural Revolution they were nicknamed the "stinking number nine." The Communist Party had identified a list of eight enemies of the people, who had long been class enemies: landowners, rich peasants, counter-revolutionaries, bad elements, rightists, renegades, enemy agents, and "capitalist roaders." They then added a ninth category to the list—intellectuals, commonly referred to as "stinking number nine." (This list has now been reduced to four: counterrevolutionaries, enemy agents, criminals, and degenerates including speculators and profiteers.)

These intellectual "enemies" were subjected to criticism, ridicule, and physical abuse in varying degrees. I questioned one respected teacher on the benefits of his manual farm labor during this period. His response was not bitter: "Perhaps personally there was some value for me to experience what the life of a peasant is like; for the educational system it was a disaster." We heard by the grapevine of the indignities suffered by one charming old teacher—a true intellectual—who was forced to wear a dunce cap and stand in an uncomfortable position for hours at a campus dining hall to be ridiculed by the students. This followed the reopening of the college in 1972, when the student body was composed of the preferred worker and peasant class.

The Cultural Revolution was officially declared at an end in 1977. That same year the entrance exams were reintroduced, but I understand that, technically, preference is still to be given to children of peasants, workers, and those cadres and intellectuals whose background does not show antirevolutionary or exploitive tendencies. In actuality I suspect that the peasants and workers would now be a minority, since new policies are putting a high priority on scientific and academic achievement to supply experts for the projected modernization program.

Some attempts at restitution were made to people who had been unjustly accused or "struggled," but these were at best spotty, depending on the local area. Surviving victims would like to erase those painful years from their memories. The youthful, radical Red Guards of that day are now approaching staid middle age and have largely joined the establishment as solid-citizen types who are productive members of the society they were once so zealously trying to reform. One up-and-coming young teacher friend admitted he had been with the Red Guards in his midteen years, thinking he was rendering a patriotic service to Chairman Mao and the cause of a better society. Some feel remorse for involvements which resulted in destruction of irreplaceable ancient relics or violence against other human beings. They were a product of their time, a time which is now looked upon with disapproval and regret.

Renewed Efforts to Catch Up

Colleges and universities and educational authorities are trying to make up for lost time. Deleted programs are being restored; postgraduate courses are gradually reappearing, foreign exchanges are being encouraged, more funds are being allocated for new textbooks, scientific materials, and expanded research. The current mood is one of optimism and hope mixed with a realistic assessment of the gigantic proportions of the task of providing democratic education for a huge population with limited facilities.

Statistics are hard to verify, especially for the rapidly changing past few years. In 1978 some statistics claimed that 90 percent of primary-age children were enrolled in school.

Other educators say somewhere between 50 and 90 percent. Whichever is true, planners accept it as an area which still needs some effort. Children go to school six days a week for about ten months of the year over a period of five years. Educators hope to return to the six years of the original plan as well as to upgrade teacher training. Many primary teachers are "irregular" teachers, not fully qualified. Quite a few students at "our" college had been such irregular teachers and were back in school preparing to be assigned as

Chinese students in their classroom. The government is allocating more funds for education to meet the need for modernization.

regular teachers. Of the primary-school graduates, 80 to 90 percent in the cities are expected to go on to middle school, 60 to 70 percent in the countryside.

Middle school is divided into three years of lower (junior) middle and two years of upper (senior) middle. Only four percent of the middle-school graduates can go on to college at this point. Of those who take the entrance exams only one out of 16 has a chance to be admitted. Those who make it receive free tuition, lodging, books, and a stipend for food and pocket money. Medical care is also said to be free, but at our college students paid a minimal fee for medications at the clinic.

Colleges and universities are upgrading their programs. The government is committed to allocating more funds for education to meet the needs of modernization. English has become the favored foreign language, with many enrolled in that department in anticipation of scientific and technical exchanges with the United States and other Western nations. My class of teachers who wanted to improve their English contained quite a few who had formerly taught Russian but in light of present reality were being "recycled" to become English teachers. (The Russian language is not very popular at present.) Technical education is being made available to workers through spare-time courses, correspondence schools, TV schools, and short-term courses. Factories encourage workers to take advantage of such classes in order to improve their skills and productivity.

Physical Culture Plays a Role

Mao's principle of all-around development stated that education should enable students to "develop morally, intellectually and physically" so that they might become workers with both socialist consciousness and culture.

Political instruction begins in first grade and continues throughout, to instill the correct moral attitudes along with intellectual growth. Physical development is one of the obvious aspects of Chinese everyday life, not just within the school system. We have already noted the emphasis on physical fitness on a college campus. An early morning traveler observes it on the still-dark streets of any city as citizens are out jogging or doing calisthenics or tai ji at street side, in parks or open areas. Physical fitness shows up in the ease with which huge loads are moved on handcarts or bicycles and in the heavy manual labor performed on construction jobs and communes. It is especially surprising to us when the muscle power is provided by a relatively petite female worker.

Physical culture plays an important part in the school curriculum at all levels, and sports of many kinds are very popular. Sports are not engaged in purely for recreation but are considered a part of the moral and social training, inculcating the team spirit, self-sacrifice, and cooperation needed for good citizenship. Team sports are favored over personal skill. Competition and individual expertise is downplayed; stress is placed on shared skills and cooperation. Some authorities credit the American YMCA movement of the late 19th century and early 20th with popularizing and influencing the promotion of modern sports activities. Military skills are also included as part of physical culture. The importance of physical education and sports for building the new socialist state, as well as the defense of the nation, is indicated by the fact that the central government has a Physical Culture and Sports Commission to promote and supervise this part of the national education endeavor.

Times are changing in sports as in everything else. In spite of protestations that sports are for citizenship- and body-building, not for competition, the Chinese take a great deal of interest in competitive sports. After being in Beijing when the world champion women's volleyball team made its triumphal return, my husband thinks that sports have a definite relationship to the national self-image. There was an obvious identification of the masses with this boost to the national ego and pride. This is 1981!

The Health of a Nation Is Important

Health care merits high priority in the PRC for the same nation-building reasons as physical culture. Public health in China in 1949 was in a precarious state, with widespread infectious diseases, nutritional deficiencies and starvation, high child mortality, and a shortage of medical personnel. Since that time the new China has focused on making the socialized health-care system available to the entire population, giving precedence to preventive medicine over curative, promoting both traditional medicine and modern Western medicine, supplying less skilled paramedics (barefoot doctors) to serve the large rural populations instead of highly trained medical personnel, who tend to concentrate in the cities. The new government launched mass campaigns to mobilize the people for active participation in needed reforms. Such campaigns included mass immunization programs to control communicable diseases and programs to eradicate venereal diseases, to exterminate disease-carrying pests, to end the extremely high incidence of drug addiction, to improve sanitation conditions, and to reduce the birth rate by family planning. I've already mentioned the public conversion to the use of boiled water, a laudable feat. (Now if someone could just launch a successful campaign to stop spitting on the floors and walks!)

In China's rural areas health care administration is the

responsibility of the communes or brigades, which provide hospitals, clinics, and public health personnel such as doctors, paramedics, midwives, and nurses to the millions previously unreached by medical help. About 1½ million barefoot doctors take basic health care, first-aid treatment, information on prevention of disease, sanitation, and hygiene to the farms and villages. These practitioners, who are only junior middle school or senior middle school graduates, are trained in commune or county hospitals or training schools for periods of up to one year. This period of instruction is followed by some practical clinical preparation. Later the paramedics may be sent for refresher courses or more specialized training. I read of one commune system which provides one barefoot doctor for every 378 rural inhabitants. Half of these barefoot doctors are women. Cases which cannot be dealt with by the paramedics are referred to brigade clinics or commune hospitals. These local medics do not receive a salary but are paid by their production teams in work points (see chapter 8).

Socialized health care is not completely free to everyone. The cost depends upon the fringe benefits supplied by the workplace. Some brigades provide free care to their members; others charge each member a fee of two or three yuan per year (three yuan would be $2.00), certainly a minimal sum. From teachers in my class I learned that the costs of childbirth are not the same for everyone. However, contraceptives, abortions, and family planning information are free to all in order to encourage family limitation.

Promotion of Physical and Mental Health

Remarkable progress has been achieved in the last 30 years, but leaders are aware that much more should be done. They are attempting to upgrade the training of barefoot doctors and other health workers. Western medicine is being promoted, but the time-tested herbal remedies are not being abandoned. The Chinese practiced herbal medicine over 3,000 years ago. By 1000 BC they had a medical administration with a system of examinations for doctors. The accumulated knowledge is still thought to be useful. Acupuncture, known as early as 500 BC, has attracted a great deal of curiosity and interest on the part of Westerners. The ancient art is still practiced. For our observation on a field trip to the Medical College in Chengdu, officials tried to schedule an operation using acupuncture anesthesia. This method is suitable for only certain types of cases, and none was on the docket for that particular time. We were, however, shown a videotape of an operation for a brain tumor using acupuncture anesthesia. It was extremely interesting for those who can tolerate that sort of carving. We were allowed to witness an operation for a stomach tumor by regular anesthetic from the safe distance of the student observation gallery right over the operating table.

Medical colleges, also closed during the Cultural Revolution, are attempting to extend the training period for medical education, to strengthen and enrich their programs. They are interested in exchanges with Western medical institutions. Most Asian hospitals are drab, dingy, and poorly equipped compared with our gleaming, antiseptic, computerized facilities. But skillful and dedicated physicians and surgeons are serving the people as best they can in their profession, which is modestly remunerated according to our standards. A large number of Chinese doctors are women.

Mental health is receiving increasing attention in China. The work of psychologists and psychiatrists was rejected by the ultraleft of the Cultural Revolution, but they are now back at work. There are mental health problems in China although their incidence of mental illness is comparatively low. Mental patients are cared for mainly in psychiatric wings of general hospitals, but there is a movement to develop community mental health centers and do more preventive work in this field. Medical colleges recognize the need to train more personnel to deal with an increasing number of cases. That China has had fewer emotional problems in the past may be due to the strong support of family and community groups, or to less stress in the predominantly rural society. With the coming of modernization and industrial development, their problems may increase. One psychiatrist noted that there are more problems among the highly skilled workers. He also made the observation that the earlier deep dedication to serve people and work for the good of others is now changing among the younger generation, and he fears this may create additional emotional problems.

Any Religious Influence?

To the casual observer it would seem that the Chinese communists have instilled in their citizens morals and ideals in a way that would be the envy of many religious groups. Religion has often been less successful in building caring communities. After discounting the element of compulsion, there still remains strong evidence of willing conformity to a sacrificial service life-style for the good of the entire society. Neither a theologian nor a philosopher, I can only ask, "Why?" Are there factors in China's long history which have eased the drastic change in the 20th-century Chinese world view? We have already seen that Confucianism was a major influence in traditional Chinese life. Chinese communists have rejected Confucianism as reactionary and counterrevolutionary, saying that it demands adherence to a conservative status quo and is based on the exploitation of the poor and powerless majority classes by an elite and powerful minority class. The reaction against the bitterness of life in the imperial past has, no doubt, strengthened the people's determination to throw all of their energies into the transformation of the system. Their dedication to the cause approaches religious fervor in a country which claims to have no interest in religion.

It is difficult to evaluate the role of religions in China's history as scholars in the past have assumed little significance attached to religion. But some are now questioning this assumption. There are some indications of a pervasive religious influence in traditional society. Its remnants are even today evident in the many temples, pagodas, monasteries, and shrines which dot the landscape all over China. The large and artistic buildings, now well maintained and preserved as historic relics, signal the importance they once held in the lives of common people. Other clues are found in the popular festivals, legends, and folk stories; the religious allusions in classical literature; the symbolism in art and architecture. Superstitions and taboos lingering in the lives of the villagers echo the religious rites of bygone days; they are not the product of organized religion but a collected heritage of ancient religious responses assimilated into the culture.

China has always been a multireligious country, but all religions have been foreign imports except for traditional (classical) religion and Taoism. Throughout the long sweep of the empire, classical religion, with its attention to the worship of heaven and lesser deities along with ancestor worship, played an important role in the relationships of people to each other and to their rulers. Confucianism, more a philosophy than a religion, in ancient imperial China replaced the function of religion with its moral and ethical system of thought forming the rules for everyday life and behavior. Taoism, springing from the teachings of a philosopher (Lao Zi) thought to be a contemporary of Confucius, evolved into a religion for the masses, who believed in its nature gods and whose lives were ordered by its superstitions and magic. Many of the secret societies which fomented rebellions against the emperors were related to Taoism.

Buddhism, imported from India, became so well assimilated in China that its ordinary followers consider it to be a native Chinese religion. It had by far the greatest following and, as we learned earlier, at one time threatened to become the state religion. Its concepts of nonviolence, compassion, and selflessness conformed well to the service motif in the new socialist society. Perhaps because of its large number of adherents, it has been more rigidly restrained than Islam and Christianity with their fewer, less threatening numbers. Islam has received the most liberal treatment by the state and has been the most active in recent years. As we have noted, it is the religion of minority groups, whose right to worship is guaranteed for the sake of unity and to keep the loyalty of Islamic citizens who occupy the strategic border regions.

Traces of a Peace Motif

Christianity, the smallest and most recent import, would tend to reinforce the service ethic and many other moral values espoused by the Chinese state. Chinese Christians are aware of the influence their religious beliefs might bring to bear in achieving the desired social ideals. They have made a considered decision to work with the state where its objectives overlap with Christian goals. They see this opportunity to work for the welfare of the poor and the oppressed and against crime and immorality as their Christian duty as well as a witness and service to fellow citizens.

Perhaps they can expand the peace theme expressed by some of their literary ancestors. Peace and nonviolence are values which make their appearance in Chinese literature. Even dynastic rulers considered violence a last resort and a tacit admission that they were losing the mandate of heaven by engaging in it. An ancient military classic of the fourth century BC stated that "the acme of skill in warfare is to subdue the enemy without fighting." The objective was the enemy's submission, not his destruction. While China has had thousands of years of internal strife and warfare, she still likes to consider herself peaceable and uninterested in "hegemony"—the dominant influence or authority of one nation over another. Many poets did deal with wars and patriotic themes, but there is a bright thread of nonviolence running through the literary tapestry—compassion for the victims of war and yearnings for peace. The eighth-century poet Du Fu spoke of the longing for peace in a poem entitled "On Washing Weapons":

> I dream that there might come some great man, who
> would bring down the River of Heaven
> cleaning all the weapons of blood,
> so that they could be stored away
> forever, never to be used again!

In the new China I was impressed with the spirit of mutuality, concern for others, cooperation, and diligence in their search for a better life. I wish them much success in that search. At the same time, I hope that they will not become so successful that they will cease to "serve the people."

6
We Go to Church

We knew we would be asked on our return to the United States, "Has the church survived in China? Did you meet any Christians? What has happened to the work of Christian missionaries?" There is probably no aspect of the new China about which Americans have been more curious than that of the current state of religion in a nation which takes obvious pride in the accomplishments of its communist government. It is an interesting fact that while one-fourth of the world's population is Chinese and one-fourth is Christian, there has been very little overlap of these billion-people segments. Christians have never numbered more than one-half of one percent of the population in China, but they have had considerable influence for such a tiny fraction.

Many Americans who see their own country as a "Christian nation" find it impossible to believe that the church could survive under a Marxist system, which historically has been diametrically opposed to religion. It is well known that Marxists have referred to religion as the opiate of the people, a superstitious reliance on superhuman powers which prevents the development of their own human potential. Expectations of perfection in the life to come promotes a lethargy which runs counter to the need to take charge of their own lives in the present world. Man can by his own efforts improve himself and his environment, eventually bringing about the "new man" and the new, just society. This is the Marxist view; most Americans find it unrealistic, to say the least.

It is also well known that most communist regimes have not been content to wait for religions to die out naturally because they are no longer needed, but have taken measures to hasten the dying process. So there is great curiosity about the effects of 30 years of communist rule on religions—especially Christianity.

The Missionary Connection

Another reason for this keen interest is that for many Americans their only contact with the China of the past was through the missionary effort. In the 19th century and first half of the 20th, many denominations took advantage of the "open door" to China afforded by the increased trade and commerical ventures, as noted in a previous chapter. We are told that already in 1922 there were 8,000 Western missionaries in China. Many mission workers and many church dollars were invested in the task of evangelizing and building institutions such as hospitals, schools, homes for the aged, orphanages, and publishing houses. These supporting churches are now truly concerned about what has happened to their investments, both temporal and spiritual.

Finally, Americans wonder what sort of society could evolve without the tempering influences of Christian principles and ethics, to which we credit the success of our own democratic and free-enterprise system. Even those who are not practicing Christians themselves like to think of our country as founded and functioning on Christian principles and moral standards in spite of our adherence to the ideal of separation of church and state.

The New China

With this background and because in our China sojourn we were representatives of a church-related college, we, too, wanted to explore the church in present-day China. We knew that Chengdu 30 years earlier had been something of a center for Christian missions. Our own Mennonite missionaries had done their language study here. Here the famous West China Union University had been founded by Canadian and U.S. mission bodies. (It is now a top-notch medical college.) Here were located mission churches of the major denominations.

Chengdu is situated in western China, which had been a haven of retreat for the missionaries and their institutions as other areas of the country fell to the communists or the Japanese in the late 30's and 40's. Foreign imperialism had

Pastor Li in the refurbished Protestant church in Chengdu.

been more associated with the seaboard cities and those strategically located along the trade routes, and for a while the foreign institutions found refuge here in the remote province of Sichuan.

We had been told by a friend—a Methodist bishop and former missionary in China—about a dear colleague and Christian brother whom we might contact in Chengdu. But how, in this huge city with its multitude of indecipherable street names and alleys? Knowing that in the past Christians had been put into jeopardy by association with foreigners, we wished to be discreet in attempting to make contacts with local people. While churches in some of the largest cities had reopened in 1979 and 1980, we were unsure about those in Chengdu. The several Chinese teachers from whom we inquired were not able to tell us since they were not Christians.

First Visit to the Protestant Church

After we were well oriented to daily routine, we decided to go directly to the college officials responsible for the foreign exchange program. They didn't know either but said they would find out. Very shortly they informed us that, yes, two Christian churches had opened—a Catholic church in the fall of 1979 and a Protestant church in March of 1980. They were ready to take all of us to visit the church whenever we wished to go. We thought it better to meet with the pastor before taking our whole group to a Sunday service. My observation that they might not appreciate a bunch of American imperialists attending a worship service, was greeted by our interpreter as extremely hilarious. His assured response was, "Of course, you would be welcomed; Americans are now our friends!" But we were not as sure as he was and still preferred a personal initial contact.

So our students along with some Chinese staff were loaded on our bus as for a field trip and taken to the church on a Saturday morning. The building, which had been confiscated by the government during the chaos of the Cultural Revolution, had been restored to the church some months before, but at the time of our visit it was in the process of a major redecorating and renovation project. The congregation was meeting in two rooms of another building, which housed the church office and was within the church compound.

Our group was warmly received by a silver-haired elder pastor and his wife, and a young lay pastor and his wife, all of whom spoke excellent English. We soon discovered that the elder pastor was none other than the former co-worker whom our bishop friend had suggested we try to locate. What a happy coincidence for us and for him! He was glad for firsthand news of his old friend, with whom he had kept some contact, but writing letters had become a difficult task in his now busy life. Pastor Li had himself been a Methodist pastor during the missionary era. He was still a pastor but no longer a Methodist, as we would soon learn.

A Postdenominational, Noninstitutional Church

Over the inevitable and hospitable cups of hot "flower" tea, Pastor Li told us of the situation of the local Christians. Whereas before the revolution Chengdu had had seven Protestant denominations, they were now united into one Christian church. Six pastors of the former disparate groups now cooperated in shepherding the flock which was being regathered as members learned that public worship was again acceptable.

Yes, there had been some doubt as to whether this merging could be done harmoniously, but it had thus far worked out very well. Even the Catholics, formerly their enemies, Pastor Li told us, were now their friends. The building which was being rehabilitated for corporate worship here was the former Anglican church. The other properties which had been turned back to the church by the government were being used to provide income for the operation of the church. The Chinese pastors were proud of their church being able to support itself. With the rental from its properties and the offerings of its members, the church does not need to accept a subsidy from the state even for the payment of pastors' salaries.

Our Chinese hosts continued to answer the questions of a thoroughly engrossed audience of Americans and Chinese. Along with their wives, Pastor Li and the young lay pastor, who is an English-language teacher at the medical college,

The members of this Protestant church in Chengdu met in two rooms of a house while their church building was being restored.

impressed us as sincere Christians committed to serving their Lord and fellow Christians in Chengdu as they rebuild, and provide leadership for, the organized church in this urban community. For our part, the best we could offer were several favorite hymns by our young American "congregation." These were received by our new friends with tears of joy!

We were assured of a warm welcome at their Sunday services. However, knowing that as many as 70 people would be crowding into these two small rooms where 30 of us were now comfortably seated, we agreed among ourselves to come in groups of only three or four each Sunday. These Chinese brothers and sisters had already waited too long for the privilege of worshiping together. We did not wish to deprive them of the limited space. Our intentions were good, and we tried to practice this plan for the duration of our stay. What we had not anticipated was the interest of the Chinese students who wished to accompany our students, so we came in greater numbers than we had expected.

Warm Welcome to Americans and Chinese

This interest in religion had surfaced early on as our students interacted with the students of the English department and as they assisted in teaching English. Many difficult questions were put to the young Americans: "Do you really believe in God? How can you believe in God when you are an educated person? May I see your Bible? Read us a story from the Bible. Do you pray? Let me hear you pray." Now, here was an opportunity to observe a Christian worship service. Whether out of curiosity, a real interest in learning more, or both, they were welcomed by the pastors and the local Christians. Some were seriously seeking and apparently finding a faith which appealed to them.

Toward the end of our stay the congregation had increased from 70 to 160, had moved into their church building, and almost filled it to capacity. We were told that as the numbers increase more churches will be opened but on a nondenominational basis. Given travel conditions in the city, it seems much more logical to have churches established on a regional basis rather than along denominational lines as of old. In a sprawling city of two or three million without private cars, it may take hours on a bicycle or crowded city bus to meet for that short Sunday morning hour with fellow believers. In the city of Nanjing, where in 1949 there were 35 churches with a total membership of 500, there were by 1958 only 4 churches serving the same number of members. In the postdenominational age the few resources must be used economically. This pattern may also do away with some of the confusing designations which stem from the foreign denominational backgrounds. For example, there was the division of missionary spheres which put Northern Baptists in Southern China and southern Baptists in northern China!

The Foreign Shadow

Before we left Chengdu, my husband and I had another visit with the pastor and his wife. At that time he told us more of his past experiences and of his hopes for the future of the church in China. He is a second-generation Christian and a second-generation pastor. Both he and his father had worked closely with foreign missionaries. He had spent some time in the United States studying and visiting churches. He cherishes those relationships and appreciates what missionaries have contributed to the planting and nurturing of the Chinese church. Yet, at age 80, he still has painful memories of his childhood years during the heyday of

Western colonial expansionism in trade and commerce, which coincided with the growth of Christian institutions.

Because of his family's connection with foreigners, he was sometimes rejected and abused by his playmates. There was a feeling of alienation from his own people during that pe-

People gather at a Catholic church in Beijing on a Sunday morning.

riod of China's growing consciousness of foreign domination and the increasing revolutionary spirit which brought about the successful nationalist revolution and establishment of the Republic in 1911. This period was followed by more revolutionary activity and a civil war in which one side was aligned with a foreign power. To be associated with that power, considered by his countrymen as repressive and exploitive, was to bear the onus of being called a traitor to his own people and his nation. To continue to cooperate with missionaries and be labeled at best a friend of "foreign devils" and at worst an enemy agent, perhaps took a greater toll of indigenous church leaders than we are able to comprehend. The missionary movement had a denationalizing effect on its converts. A popular saying in that era was, "Win a convert; lose a citizen." It was difficult to conceive of a really loyal Chinese committing his life to a foreign religion.

In the first few years following the establishment of the People's Republic of China, most foreign missionaries left or were expelled from China. The infant church was left to "sink or swim." In analyzing the situation since liberation (1949), Chinese church leaders generally divide the experience into three periods: (1) the postrevolution years from 1949 to 1966, (2) the Cultural Revolution years from 1966 to 1976, and (3) the current period of moderation since 1976.

Period of Adjustment

During the first years the church had to make a great adjustment to the new realities of a socialist society. It was in this period that the church became de-institutionalized as well as postdenominational. In the first place, both Western personnel and mission board dollars were withdrawn from the many institutions which had been established. While some missions had conscientiously tried to prepare Chinese for leadership positions, it was more or less inevitable that major responsibility remained in the hands of the sponsoring and funding agency. Chinese church groups would have been unable to take over financial and personnel support of the many educational and welfare institutions in operation at that time had they been granted that option.

Such an option was not likely to be offered them. The ideal socialist society supplies all physical needs as well as the motivation and direction required by the "new socialist man," who is committed to work for the good of all the people and the advancement of the nation. The masses must look to the party to fulfill all their needs. People could not be recipients of charity from an elitist group or from religious groups which would draw allegiance to themselves instead of to the state. Therefore, all institutions were taken over by the government and operated to provide the same services or adapted to what they felt were needed for the welfare of the new society.

There was much uncertainty about how the church should react to a communist government. Older church leaders readily confess to many doubts, partially because of their indoctrination to Western thinking about the evils innate in communism as an atheistic system of control with no redeeming features. Because of what they now call misinformation and misunderstanding, they were not prepared to expect freedom of religion even though the new constitution specifically stated that "citizens shall enjoy freedom to believe in religion or not to believe in religion" (1954 constitution, article 46). But when these leaders began to see the government seriously, and successfully, working at elimination of hunger and starvation, illiteracy, prostitution, disease, and oppression, it became apparent to them that many of socialism's objectives overlapped with their own aspirations for the poor and oppressed masses in China. They came to see the church's position as one of cooperation with the government for the accomplishment of those goals.

Church and State Goals Overlap

Chinese Christians in general today take a positive attitude toward the new China and see their role as a supportive one, to gain objectives which they consider parallel to Christian values. They welcome a social system which is able to raise the moral and physical level of life. They see the party's injunction to "serve the people" as equivalent to the scripture's injunction to "love your neighbor." They find many of China's values to be Christian—cooperation, honesty, morality, self-sacrifice, service, egalitarianism, productive work, modesty, and simple life-style. They see an opportunity for themselves to be models in Chinese society—in schools, offices, factories, on the farm and in the home; they can make a witness by living out their Christian principles.

Joseph Needham, a British scientist and a Christian, thinks that China has found ways of living which are basically the same as the Christian way. The paradox is that while rejecting the first commandment, the Chinese are implementing the second great commandment far better than has ever been done by Christendom. (Raymond L. Whitehead and Rhea M. Whitehead, *China: Search for Community*).

An added incentive for Chinese Christians to work for the nation's interests was the need to prove their patriotism. China's entry into the Korean War hastened the end of mission involvement and intensified the need to prove their loyalty. Their former American colleagues were now the enemy on the battlefield, and the danger of being considered enemy agents was even more serious.

As early as 1950, Protestant leaders, after meeting with Premier Zhou Enlai, issued a manifesto which set forth the political stance of the Christians in the new China. This document called for a separation from the "imperialistic influences" of the past and encouraged the government's policy of reform, opposing war and upholding peace. Members were asked to actively promote self-respect and self-reliance through the Three-Self Movement (which will be discussed shortly) and to cultivate a patriotic and democratic spirit. The manifesto also called for emphasis on a deeper understanding of Christianity, a closer unity among denominations, and participation in the work of building a socialist society through service to the people, by productive labor and correct teaching.

The Chinese view their patriotic stance as the natural feelings of a citizen for the homeland. One Catholic sister is reported to have said that she felt a second liberation when she began to see the responsibility of Christians to work with the people in their striving for a better life, rather than to remain aloof. The Old Testament prophets loved the people of their country; Jesus loved the common people; Paul was proud of his citizenship. The church's work and witness, she felt, is rightly out in the world, not within its own cloistered walls.

They also insist that their patriotism is real and not something they are pretending in order to preserve the life of the church. Patriotism does not demand blind praise of everything and does not exclude opportunity for prophetic witness where change is needed.

In 1950 the government established a Bureau of Religious Affairs to relate to the various religious groups in the PRC. Its duty is to serve as liaison between the religious bodies and the government, to interpret government policy concerning religion. Some critics have charged that its function is to re-educate the religious leaders and believers to obtain their cooperation in the development of socialism and to neutralize reactionaries within the religious communities. Chinese church leaders tend to describe the bureau not as a supervisory body but as an agency of the state to assist in implementing religious freedom, to negotiate for the churches in obtaining needed supplies, such as the paper which is used for the printing of Bibles and religious materials.

Perhaps the real purpose of the Bureau of Religious Affairs encompasses both types of service, for the state and for the church. In any case, from the beginning the communist government has taken pains to establish a mutual working relationship with the religious groups in the context of its united front policy. This policy seeks the support of all facets of society, including religious groups and minorities, emphasizing the commonalities rather than differences, so that all may contribute toward achieving the state's goals. The bureau has played an important role in preserving the guaranteed rights of the church such as exemption from taxes and freedom of belief—rights which might be denied by local authorities or antireligious elements in society without this watchdog over the relations of church and state.

The Three-Self Movement—Whose Idea?

Another organization which facilitates working with the state is the Chinese Protestant Three-Self Patriotic Movement, which was organized in 1951. Here again there are differences in opinion as to whether this association was organized at the behest of the state or whether it was a spontaneous outgrowth of the needs of the postliberation church. Bishop K. H. Ting, chief spokesman for the Chinese Protestants and chairperson of the Three-Self Movement, denies that the Communist Party ordered the church to organize such a body. He does say, however, that they received appreciation and encouragement from Premier Zhou Enlai (*China Notes*, Winter 1980-81).

Actually, for those who see the Three-Self Movement as a communist conspiracy to control the church, it should be pointed out that the idea originated among missionaries already in the last half of the 19th century. Some of their number were concerned about training indigenous leaders of mission churches to be able to take over the conduct of the work themselves. In other words, these farsighted missionaries were interested in "working themselves out of a job" rather than in promoting dependency upon themselves. For the most productive use of foreign personnel and for the health of the young churches, this was a sound policy. The report of General Conference Mennonite missionaries in China at a 1922 conference states, "The great aim of all our work is a self-supporting, self-controlling, self-propagating church" (Matilda K. Voth, *Clear Shining After Rain*, p. 86).

To completely carry this out was difficult with the strictures of mission agencies and the need to give an account of time and funds to boards back home. But China in the 50's was an ideal place for the experiment. The Chinese church was put into a position where the three selfs (self-support, self-government, self-propagation) were the key to survival, or the alternative to extinction. Farsighted leaders saw that a religion linked with, or having remnants of, the hated foreign imperialism would have little appeal for prospective Chinese converts. To evangelize others, or even to cling to their own faith, they would have to find a way of making their religion indigenous. A Christianity that would be financed, administered, and propagated by Chinese themselves offered hope of salvaging the infant church. Only such a church would be acceptable to the masses of the people, that vast field for evangelization.

Early Uncertainty

Some could not go along with this movement, seeing it as a compromise with the separation of church and state principle. While the government had apparently been circumspect in its provisions for religious belief and practice, the church people in those early years were still fearful and did not trust taking any steps which might make them vulnerable to attack or discrimination. The communist line was still in favor of atheism, and efforts were made to educate all Chinese to that belief. Mao Zedong, in the early years of the communist revolution, had gone on record as being opposed to the use of force against religion, acknowledging that an ideology cannot be changed by force. He strongly believed that religion would simply become obsolete in a society where it was no longer needed. Then people would give it up voluntarily. In 1927 he wrote, "It is the peasants who made the idols and when the time comes they will cast the idols aside with their own hands" (Robert G. Orr, *Religion in China*, p. 32). He was prepared to wait; as it turned out he had a long, long wait. But he still stuck to his belief that religions could not be eliminated by force. In 1957, in his essay "On the Correct Handling of Contradictions Among the People," he wrote:

> We cannot abolish religion by administrative orders; nor can we force people not to believe in it. We cannot compel people to give up idealism, any more than we can force them to believe in Marxism. In settling matters of ideological nature or controversial issues among the people, we can only use democratic methods, methods of discussion, of criticism, of persuasion and education, not coercive, high-handed methods.

In spite of these pronouncements, in the 50's Christians could not quite believe that the communists were really allowing them freedom of belief. It was only later, in the period of persecution, that they could look back on those years as having presented opportunities which they had failed to fully exploit. Many people became "closet" Christians, worshiping secretly in their own homes and without connection to the emerging church establishment. The public church continued to function with some inhibitions but did make adaptations to the new situation, setting up structures for its maintenance, as we have noted.

Catholics Have More Members and More Problems

We have said little about the Catholic Church although it is much the larger of the two groups. In 1949 it had about three million members compared to 700,000 for the Protestant churches. In many respects Catholics have had a more difficult time than Protestants. In the first place it was more difficult, next to impossible, for them to dissociate themselves from a foreign entity. To remain authentically Catholic they had to maintain relationships with the pope—a foreign church official—and the Vatican—a foreign political power which has continued to recognize the Nationalist regime on Taiwan.

Secondly, Catholic missionaries were not generally recalled in 1950 as were Protestants, but were ordered to stay at their posts. Many did leave during the Korean War, and almost all had left by 1956 except those who were in prison. They were more openly resistant to a communist government than Protestants had been. As a result, there were conflicts and harsh treatment of both foreign and Chinese priests. Many were imprisoned and more than a few put to death. Many priests were actively opposing the state and refusing to allow their members to cooperate in the united front.

Most Catholics were at first adamant in their refusal to organize a counterpart to the Protestant Three-Self Movement. It was not until 1954 that the National Patriotic Catholic Association got any degree of support, and not until 1960 did it really get under way. One reason for this resistance was the lack of an indigenous hierarchy or priesthood, the great majority of those positions being held by foreigners. Another problem was that the break with the Roman Church would produce a schismatic church no longer the true church.

So it was with a great deal of agonizing that Catholics reorganized their churches separate from Rome, ordained bishops not recognized by the pope, and, in effect, accepted a role in the united front effort to build a socialist society. This portion of the Catholic Church is the one recognized by the state as the Chinese Catholic Church. However, there are still people who refuse to sever their connections with the Vatican. They comprise a group of unknown size, which a visiting European cardinal recently referred to as the "catacomb church."

For the most part, Catholics are hoping for the normalization of relations between China and the Vatican. It remains to be seen whether Pope John Paul II will be able to take steps in that direction. Meantime, Catholic churches are reopening, and, like Protestants, they are making preparations to train younger leaders and provide pastoral care for their far-flung membership.

The Cultural Revolution Brought Suffering

The second period which Chinese Christians faced was that of the Great Proletarian Cultural Revolution from 1966 to 1976. These years were a time of uncontrolled chaos and the near collapse of the PRC, a time of great suffering for many people and a time of severe trial for Chinese Christians.

In the summer of 1966, Mao Zedong unleashed millions of his Red Guards, drawn from university and high school students across the country, with his blessing to carry out "revolution." By this time the Mao cult had reached the stage where the nod of the master became the command of the masses. The rationale for reviving the revolution was that new elites were appearing in the leadership, there was a crisis in the effort of achieving equality for all in a classless society, and leaders were less radical and had lost their vision for the new society which was a necessary step toward the ultimate ideal communist state. Underneath this rhetoric of a "greening" of the old revolutionary spirit for the good of the masses was a political power struggle among the top leaders, with Mao fearful of losing control of the party.

The youthful and idealistic Red Guards responding to Mao's call were zealous in their desire to make revolution for the good of "the people." The dragons they went forth to slay were what Mao called the "four olds"—old habits, old customs, old ideas, old culture. These were the supposed impediments to achievement of the good society. Religion was not singled out as the major enemy, but it was definitely one of the many old ideas which should have been discarded by now. It was a part of the old culture assumed to be no longer needed.

It was inevitable that in the fury of the Red Guard struggle to suppress the "four olds," Christians would be prime targets. The Bureau of Religious Affairs was closed down, religious buildings were confiscated and closed or used for secular purposes, individual Christians were persecuted, leaders were imprisoned, religious books and literature were burned, shrines and holy places of all religions were desecrated or vandalized, some private homes were stripped of valuable belongings, and adherents to religious beliefs were sent to re-education schools to correct their thinking and attitudes toward revolution.

Christians Most Vulnerable

Of all religious groups Christians were most vulnerable to harassment because they carried the stigma of a foreign religion and association with an enemy nation. During the Cultural Revolution nine categories of Chinese were listed as "enemies of the people": landowners, rich peasants, counterrevolutionaries, bad elements, rightists, renegades, enemy agents, "capitalist roaders," and intellectuals. Christians tended to fall into several of these categories, thus were in double (or triple) jeopardy. Because of their working relations with Westerners, they could be labeled capitalist roaders. If they had American friends, relatives, or other connections, they might be enemy agents. Because Christian missions had put emphasis on education, many of them were educated—thus guilty of being intellectuals. Their Christian teachings may have inhibited their enthusiasm for violence and revolution, making them counterrevolutionaries. We must keep in mind, however, that there were also non-Christians in all these categories, lest we see the atrocities of the Cultural Revolution purely as a vendetta against Christians.

A pastor told us of his own treatment during this period. He spent some time in prison. His precious library of Christian books, many of them in English and irreplaceable, was completely destroyed. Household furnishings were appropriated by the Red Guards. A dedicated and competent

Christian doctor of our acquaintance spent years in prison, often in solitary confinement. She had studied in the United States and maintained many friends and contacts there. After years of medical work in a prison camp, she has finally been restored to professional status in a hospital, where at age 78 she is head of a department. Another respected medical specialist was placed under house arrest in his hospital and forced to undergo "criticism and struggle." He, too, had studied in the United States, had an American wife, and his children were living outside China. He and his wife were subjected to midnight searches of their home, their personal possessions, papers, and correspondence. He was also reinstated to good standing in his profession and at his death in the spring of 1980 given a state funeral with great honors because of his outstanding contributions in the medical field.

Treatment of Cultural Revolution victims varied with the locality and the amount of control exercised by the legitimate authorities. But probably very few Christian families escaped some harassment, and many underwent severe persecution. Often their young people were sent to the countryside to engage in "productive labor" and re-education. It is said that Bishop Ting, a national church leader and member of the National People's Congress, had to spend some time in reform through labor. Almost all schools and colleges were closed from 1966 to 1972, causing a serious gap in the education of future church leaders.

During these traumatic years many Christians continued their worship and fellowship with other believers in small groups meeting in homes. Some of these secret meetings consisted of only family members; others were with trusted friends or neighbors. Even the matter of trust was a nebulous element. We are told that some families were fearful of imparting their religious faith to their own children because of the danger of being reported in criticism sessions. Many of these house churches are still meeting, either in addition to public worship or because public worship places are not yet open or are too remote.

The most violent and destructive phase of the Cultural Revolution declined in 1969 and 1970 although it was not officially terminated until after Mao's death in 1976. The power struggle ended with the moderates taking control. In 1980 the Chinese people were freely discussing this aberration in their national aspirations for a better life. There were many forcefully asserting that it could never happen again. Yet those who remember the pain of the past are reluctant to expose themselves too soon to the fluctuations of an uncertain future. When in the late 70's China began to reach out to other countries and slowly unlocked its doors to foreign visitors, new hope was given to religious groups, an optimism much in evidence among church leaders.

Wanted: An Indigenous Church

This brings us to the third phase of the church's sojourn in a communist land. From 1979 to 1981 changes have occurred so rapidly that it is difficult to make an appraisal of the situation at any given time. What seems true today may be either reinforced or negated by what happens tomorrow.

While it appears that the church was never dead, even in its darkest hours, it is now emerging with renewed strength and vigor but without complete freedom to reconstruct and expand activities. Christians remain a tiny minority of less than one-half of one percent of the total population. In spite of the loss of some who rejected their faith under the pressures of the Cultural Revolution, the inability to actively evangelize, and the natural attrition by death, church leaders are confident that today they have more believers than before liberation. Estimates place the number at one million Protestants and three million Catholics.

Pastors now feel that those bitter years were ones of testing and refining. They brought much suffering but resulted in a purification process which leaves the church stronger. Even though many did give up their faith, many new believers were added because of the remarkable witness of Christians who remained true in the face of persecution. In May 1981 it was said that 80 churches were open for public worship. By August, we read, that figure had doubled. Week by week more are added. These are filled to overflowing, and new members are being baptized.

Some of our group attended midnight mass in the Catholic cathedral in Shanghai on Christmas eve of 1980. They were surprised to find a crowd of 5,000 devoutly celebrating this joyous occasion. Given the transportation possibilities, the mere logistics of so many people converging on one spot within this sprawling city in the middle of the night was impressive. The service was also impressive.

On the Sunday after Christmas my husband and I attended a worship service at Mo-en (formerly Moore Memorial) Church in Shanghai. We arrived at 10:00 for the 10:30 service to find a congregation of 2,000 already in the pews, practicing their singing while they waited. The remarkable thing was that this was the third service of the morning. There had already been equally large gatherings at 6:30 and 8:30. Many churches hold multiple services, and they say that the pastor must repeat the same sermon in each; otherwise people would stay for a second round!

Here, as in our little church in Chengdu, we were conscious of an audience actively involved in the service, not passive spectators. There were evidences of affirmation—

amens, nods, tears, smiles—and deep devotion. Yes, there are many lined and weathered old faces in the pews but also many middle-aged, some youth, and a few children. At Nanjing University a three-hour lecture and discussion on the foundations of Christianity had an attendance of 1,000 students.

Plans for Renewal

Because of the age factor there is concern about future leadership. In the fall of 1980 a National Christian Conference convened in Nanjing with delegates coming from all across China. It was agreed to form a China Christian Council, which would give leadership and guidance in such areas as pastoral care, leadership training, publication of Christian literature (Bibles, theological education materials, hymnbooks, periodicals), and a new translation of the Bible. In February of 1981 the Christian Theological Seminary in Nanjing resumed its task of educating pastors with 48 students chosen from nearly 500 applicants. More than one-third of these students, ages 18 to 35, are women. The seminary has also produced a correspondence course, *Syllabus*. Issued quarterly, *Syllabus* started out with 5,000 copies, but demand was so great that subsequently 30,000 copies were printed. Most of these go to leaders of house-church groups. The China Christian Council is taking steps to help prepare the new leadership so desperately needed.

In 1980, for the first time since 1947, new Bibles came off the press. A total of 135,000 (85,000 complete Bibles and 50,000 New Testaments) were printed, and in several churches we heard it announced in December that the new Bibles were available. (More are expected to be printed in 1981.) Because of the urgency of time this was a reprinting of the old version. A new translation in modern Chinese is in process. At a press conference in Hong Kong one Chinese pastor said, "The Bible has been printed for the first time in China with Chinese money, Chinese technology, and Chinese paper." Their pride in having done it themselves is evident. There is also interest in making their hymnbooks more genuinely Chinese. The current collection is practically all Western hymns. For an American visitor there is something comforting to be able to sing along in a strange language but a familiar tune; but there is also something sad about all those Chinese voices singing European tunes. In January 1981 the China Christian Council solicited the composition of new indigenous hymns for possible use in a new book.

Church leaders have much work ahead of them in the areas mentioned earlier, as well as in strengthening their postdenominational unity, enriching their worship services and making them more truly indigenous, witnessing to non-Christians, and relating to the many small groups which will continue to meet. Chinese resent the tendency of overseas observers to consider these small groups an underground church refusing to cooperate with the organized church, or a protest against the Three-Self Movement. There may well be some who object to the church/state relationship, in which the church is working with government agencies and promoting the objectives of a socialist society based on Marxist principles. But, according to the conversations and writings of church leaders, this is not the major reason for house churches.

Small-group worship has been a part of traditional Chinese culture which still feels comfortable to many people, they say. Especially in the rural areas, church buildings have not yet been reopened; in the cities it is difficult to gather at the few public meeting places which are open.

Staggered work schedules mean that not all people have their day off on Sunday. The cost of maintaining old Western-style buildings must be considered. Such factors may keep some small groups worshiping in homes or as neighborhood groups, as a needed supplement to corporate worship, for some time to come.

When I asked a Chengdu pastor whether they would try to contact the known Christians in the city and invite them to return to the public services, he said, "No. They will return as they gain confidence and overcome the trauma of the Cultural Revolution. Those who worship in their homes for whatever reason are also faithful Christians. We will let them decide. They will return when they are ready." Chinese leaders suspect that the people outside China who portray house churches as the faithful remnant resisting communism are motivated more by political convictions than by concern for their fellow believers, thereby driving a divisive wedge rather than building up the spiritual community. Bishop Ting finds this divisive tactic unacceptable and maintains that all Chinese Protestants are citizens of the People's Republic of China, all are self-governing, self-supporting, and self-nurturing, therefore a part of the Three-Self Movement whether they meet in small groups or with the big crowds coming to the churches. Many attend both and would be offended to be called the underground church (*China Notes*, Winter 1979-80).

Significant New Experiment

From the standpoint of the long sweep of Chinese history, there is logical reason for government to fear religious groups. Buddhist, Taoist, and sometimes Christian adherents were often the seedbeds of resistance movements against political regimes in the old days of the emperors.

Government leaders are aware that religions have traditionally played a large role in the life of the common people, that in times of crisis people reach out for religion. (Today's Christians, however, are emphasizing that their faith is to be cherished in good times as well as bad.) Mao Zedong, in a report on peasant movements in 1927, cited religion as one of the three systems of authority operative among the peasants. The other two were clan authority (family and ancestors) and masculine authority (husbands and fathers).

This points up the excitement of the past 15 years in evaluating the role of Christianity in the historic events of our time. Bishop Ting has made the astonishing statement that the Chinese Christians in their response to building a socialist system in a poor country which had been semicolonial and semifeudalistic may be tremendously important to world religions. He equates its significance to that of the Reformation during the transition from European feudalism to capitalism. By a quirk of history the small church in China may be serving as a laboratory in the great experiment and entering into a new and unique stage in history where the church will play a greater role in shaping the destiny of mankind, in doing away with oppression and exploitation and establishing a more just society. Whether or not we agree with this startling analysis, in order to understand the Chinese church's situation we must be aware of their feelings and aspirations, their problems and triumphs.

So where is the church today in relation to its own grass roots, its controlling government, and its global connections? It should be pointed out that the new moderation with respect to religious practice, as well as other aspects of life in China, is perhaps motivated by several factors. With the new openness to other nations and the desire for technical and scientific aid in achieving the Four Modernizations,

China's leaders wish to present a face acceptable to those nations. Many of the industrialized countries are so-called Christian nations, and tourists from them are getting a first-hand look at China. These visitors are asking to attend worship services and are curious about the health of the church. It is no doubt true that some of the relaxation of control is politically motivated. It is part of the public relations promotion for these new cross-cultural friendships, a part of the united front approach to the great task of modernization. The pendulum is swinging back from the ultraleft extremes of the Cultural Revolution. Who knows how far it will go, or when it may sweep in the opposite direction?

Even with these reservations we must agree that current policies are a more faithful carrying out of the right of religious freedom which has always been guaranteed by the constitution. In the 1975 revision of the constitution, to the original statement that "citizens shall enjoy freedom to believe in religion or not to believe in religion" was added the phrase "and to propagate atheism." This addition has understandably worried Christians, since it appears to give atheists, but not Christians or other religions, approval for propagating their beliefs. In 1979, Christian leaders called for a return to the 1954 wording. At this point there has been no change, but the National People's Congress did make provision in a penal code that government cadres who violate the official policy of freedom of religion are liable to two years in prison. While this is an added protection, it depends much on local enforcement for its effectiveness.

There still remains some ambiguity about how much freedom Christians may exercise in evangelizing. Currently they seem to be engrossed in the huge task of regathering and nurturing their own members, providing materials and leadership training, and building up an indigenous Chinese church free of the taint of foreign domination or control. Only such a church can appeal to the masses of Chinese with their strong loyalty to the motherland and patriotic support for a more just social system. When the time comes for public evangelism, church leaders feel confident that they will be capable of doing it in a better way than could foreign missionaries. Meanwhile they see the cooperation of church members in the building of that hoped-for better society as a form of evangelism.

The Church Must Stand on Its Own Feet

We should not forget that some, perhaps innocent, efforts to evangelize from outside—whether by radio broadcast, tract distribution, Bible smuggling, or religious research—may be seen by Chinese Christians as a violation of their autonomy, infiltration, propaganda spreading, intelligence gathering (spying?), and interfering in affairs which they can very well attend to in their own way. We must respect their strong conviction that in order for the church to take root and grow in Chinese soil it must acquire an unmistakable Chinese identity. The Chinese, though they verbally kowtow to the more technically advanced nations, are a proud people. They are reluctant to accept gifts or favors from foreigners when they are unable to reciprocate.

A wary relationship with foreign Christians is beginning to emerge. As we were warmly welcomed in the worship services, so are the many other Western visitors—but as fellow worshipers, not as leaders or benefactors or power brokers. Chinese Christians are interested in ecumenical exchanges on an equal footing—as brothers and sisters, not as mother and daughter churches. One pastor said to us, "We hope the time will come when foreign guests can come to us to tell us what the Lord is doing for you; we also hope we can come to you to tell you what the Lord is doing for us in China." Can we who are so proud of our ecclesiastical expertise and our organizational know-how gracefully take a back seat? Can we humbly acknowledge the fact that God is able to work in China without our present help?

It seems obvious, and certainly valid, that any expectations of the Western church to re-enter China must be on the basis of equality, with full respect for the dignity, the capability, and the sincerity of Chinese brothers and sisters. The activities of some foreign Christians—Bible smuggling, underground evangelism, flaunting of Western economic or academic advantages, disregard for legal restrictions, or any other act which distorts the image of Christianity as universal, moral, and righteous—are a disservice to Chinese Christians.

We should evaluate our inclinations to help, and see whether our offers may violate the authority and jurisdiction of the indigenous church and how they might be interpreted by the Chinese. The last thing they need is for us to put stumbling blocks in their path! Don MacInnis, well-known China expert and former missionary, wisely counsels the Western church: "We must not overwhelm them with thoughtless generosity, nor jeopardize their hard won identity, autonomy and self-reliance" (*International Bulletin of Missionary Research,* April 1981). Bible smuggling, one form of well-intentioned help, may really have the opposite effect. It not only puts the honesty of Christians into question; it may undercut the economic viability of their publishing efforts and put them into jeopardy with government officials. The Chinese church leaders say they have no objection to outsiders sending individual copies of the Bible to relatives and friends. But their responsibility and self-reliance is threatened if Bibles come in the millions. Too often altruistic motives are mixed with political motives. The known cases of antigovernment tracts hidden in Bibles are an embarrassment to Christians and cast a shadow on their integrity.

How Can We Help?

What, then, can we do to show our concern and support? We can do a number of things while accepting the fact that they will have to do most things for themselves. We can study to be better informed on the total situation. We can offer friendship and support on a sister-church basis rather than criticism and suspicion. We can re-examine our relationship with our own social and political systems before judging Chinese adaptations to state and society. We can accept the challenge to restudy the biblical meaning of mission to the world, what it means to be *in* the world but not *of* the world, what is our responsibility to the people outside the warm fold of our own denominations. At least a few of us can take the opportunity to live out our faith as we serve in possible openings for exchange in needed areas of education, expertise, or technology. Even here we must be sensitive that we approach such "service" not from a position of power, not from self-interest, but from a position of powerlessness and with real respect for the best interests of the Chinese.

Until invited to participate in verbal evangelism or structured mission work, we can refrain from undercover strategies which erode the foundations of a truly indigenous church with its right to make its own decisions in all areas of church growth and activity, and which cast grave doubt on the sincerity of our proffered friendship. Finally, Christians are not inhibited in the practice of prayer—for the thousands of Chinese at work in building the church on *their* turf, for ourselves that we may be faithful to *our* tasks of kingdom-building.

Going to church in China was an eye-opening, faith-expanding experience. It should be exciting to see the shape of the Chinese Christian church as it emerges in the 1980's.

7

Home Life Then and Now

To walk down any street in the new China is to be aware of families and the activities associated with the home. Daily chores which we do behind closed doors are in progress out in the open. Laundry tubs at curbside, damp wash suspended from bamboo poles overhead, preparation of vegetables by the doorstep, children's games within the flow of traffic, glimpses through open doors into the small quarters which will become the haven of an incredible number of people when street busyness ceases for the day—all remind us of the importance of family life in the nurture of tomorrow's citizens. The teeming streets, shops, classrooms, and farms swarming with healthy, happy children, proud parents, and patient grandparents indicate that home life is still thriving.

Occasionally, however, a little old lady tottering along on tiny feet brings us the shocking reminder that the era of footbinding was not somewhere in the dim past but actually within the lifetime of this flesh-and-blood remnant of the old imperial China. What radical changes, what social upheaval, what pains or joys of adjustment are imprinted on her memory of only 50 or 60 years! The key to the remarkably sudden changes in family life is the drastic change in the roles of women and men in the new socialist society. The torturous practice of foot-binding displayed in the crippled feet of this elderly woman symbolizes how women were bound in other ways—bound to the hearth and private confines of the home, bound by the whims of male authority figures, bound to illiteracy and incompetence by traditional society's horror of an educated woman.

Traditional China's Extended Family

We have all read storybook accounts of the traditional extended family of three or four generations under one roof or cluster of roofs. There are enchanting aspects of such mutual support and interaction among family members. But the highly layered, male-oriented, patriarchal system opened the door to all kinds of despotism and tyranny if the all-powerful patriarch were so inclined.

The traditional family was headed by the oldest male

Americans mingle with Chinese shoppers at an outdoor market.

(grandfather or great-grandfather), his younger brothers, sons and nephews, grandsons and grandnephews, and so on depending on longevity. No, it is not a mistake that I have not mentioned daughters. Daughters were only a temporary, therefore negligible, part of the family. When a daughter married, she became a part of her husband's household. She was a negotiable product that could be used for forming alliances with another family which would enhance the economic, social, or political status of her parental family. In the meantime she was a financial drain on that family since it had to provide her material needs during the growing-up years as well as a dowry which would ensure a good match. Her years of productive labor would be given to the husband's family.

In this situation it is not surprising that girl babies were often less than welcome. A family wanted at least enough sons to balance out the daughters. Infanticide was the fate of many female infants. And the betrothal of a young girl to an old man was a possible solution to a family's financial crisis. Male children, on the other hand, were necessary to carry on the family line, to ensure the economic security of the clan, to arrange for the worship and appropriate care of the ancestral tombs. Eventually the eldest son carried the burden of responsibility for the extended family, both living and dead.

The father in this system was the supreme ruler of the family, its property, income, and members (who were a part of the property). He exerted the power of life or death over his children and wife. At his command, daughters could be disposed of through infanticide, sold into slavery, or betrothed as child brides. Even a son could be sold as a slave or put to death in case of extreme filial misconduct which might reflect adversely on the family's honor or prestige. A wife could be repudiated by her husband and sent back to her parental home, where she would become an unwelcome burden. He could divorce her peremptorily for various, sometimes frivolous, reasons, but she had no recourse in an undesirable marriage bond.

A woman had no legal status. She could not own property, could not inherit from her father or husband, had no money under her control. She was throughout her life subservient to and dependent upon a male—first her father, then her husband, and finally her sons. A widow was usually not allowed to remarry. Few daughters would resist the marriages arranged for them no matter how repugnant; it was a matter of economic survival.

A man, to look at the other side of the coin, carried a heavy burden of responsibility if he was the head of a household. Almost sole responsibility for the economic welfare of the large brood, the necessary discipline to ensure the good name of the family, arranging socially advantageous marriages for his sons and daughters, living up to the high standards of the Confucian codes for males—all these duties added up to no easy load. Of course, he took counsel with the other senior male members of the extended family. Overtly, a wife had no voice in such decisions, although it can be assumed that many wives did exercise power in devious ways. Many Chinese women were known for their strong will and good judgment.

A woman did achieve some status by giving birth to sons, the very sons to whom she would some day be subservient. She could even look forward to being able to play a dominant role when the brides of her sons were brought into the household. The tyranny of the mother-in-law was a source of much grief to many a young wife, who could only retaliate when she herself became a mother-in-law.

If a family prospered, the wife could expect other wives and concubines to be added to the household, especially if she had failed to produce a son. In general, the first wife was supposed to have a superior position above later wives or concubines and many times may have welcomed their assistance as well as their company. Since marriage was a family contract and not an individual choice, since affectional or romantic considerations were less important than the practical aspects, additional wives did not signify the personal rejection we would associate with such a practice. But it was a great disappointment and disgrace not to bear a son. The highly ritualistic marriage ceremonies included rites to ensure the blessings of the god of fertility, and the messages of friends and well-wishers centered on the hopes for many sons. But the gods were not always accommodating.

The Cultural Filter

We must not be too critical of the family system of the past. We are looking at it through glasses colored by the context of our own culture and our own age. Most fathers were, no doubt, not too much different from all human fathers and did not use the great power at their disposal to inflict unhappiness on their offspring or to become the heartless tyrants the system would have allowed. Most parents, no doubt, were concerned for the physical, moral, and social well-being of the children they had brought into existence just as today's parents are. Many Chinese, especially of the upper economic level, look back on those "bad old days" with pleasure.

One author, Chiang Yee, in stories about his growing-up years in the early 1900's, describes his landholding family of four generations all living together in the ancestral home headed by his grandfather *(Chinese Childhood)*. He depicts his childhood years as happy, his family relations as warm and comfortable, the clan spirit strong and proud. Their clan book traced the family tree from the first century BC; his branch of the clan had owned the lands of the area for 47 generations, and the present house had sheltered 10 generations. Their economic position was secure; marriage arrangements could allow some leniency to the young partners. His sister saw her intended husband and approved of the bargain; her new family was "modern" enough to want her to have some education and to allow her to make frequent visits to the ancestral home. He looks back with nostalgia to a life-style which had disappeared by World War II. But we must remember that he was looking at his early years from the privileged position of a fairly wealthy family and the male sex.

What Did Confucius Say?

The traditional family was much influenced by Confucian philosophy, which set the tone for Chinese private life as well as public life. This Confucian ethic, which shaped the social and political life from the fifth century BC to the 20th-century revolutions, placed major emphasis on proper conduct in specific relationships. The family was the basic unit of the political system, which was founded on the same doctrines of domination and status. The home molded obedient family members, who became obedient citizens. This very status conscious hierarchy placed every member into a clearly defined pigeonhole according to age, sex, and position: the domination of age over youth, male over female, and the ruler over the ruled.

The generations established a hierarchy which outlined the demands and privileges of each. Every member understood how he fit into that pattern. A young man of the third generation who had an uncle (second generation) very little or no older than himself recognized that his daily playmate was entitled to certain respect and privileges of his generation. He also knew the perquisites of his own slot in society. In general, age was always respected and shown deference.

In the matter of male dominance over females, we have already noted the practical applications and some of the reasons. In theory, it was in accord with the Confucian principle of filial obedience—children to parents, especially son to father. Moreover, much of what appears to us as discrimination against women came from the ancient Chinese world view which saw everything as the result of interaction between two forces—yin and yang. Yin was the element carrying all the supposed female traits—dark, weak, and passive. Yang carried all the male traits—bright, strong, and active. I suppose it might have been said that women's unfortunate lot was really not their fault; that was just the way the universe was formed. So the male philosophers worked out the code of behavior expected of both the passive females and the active males. This meant domination of male over female and the assignment of roles accordingly.

The theory is embodied in the "three bonds" which establish the relationship between the superior and the subordinate in the family and the state: the bond of loyalty on the part of subject to ruler (minister to emperor, lower official to higher official); the bond of filial obedience on the part of son to father (children to parents); and the bond of chastity on the part of wives but not of husbands. These doctrines did maintain an ordered society for centuries—in fact, one of the longest continuous societies ever to exist.

It is hard to evaluate the real nature of that bond of family kinship. Was the closeness affectional, or was it programmed by the strict control of behavior? Love and respect for the head of the family was often mixed with fear and awe. On the other hand, we read stories of the great love and respect for the mother even in her powerlessness. Affection was not a necessary ingredient for marriage and reproduction, but duty and obedience were highly valued. Affection among siblings was not a requirement in fulfilling the codes of filial piety, but conformity and courtesy were demanded. Loyalty to the family was ensured by a deeply ingrained sense of propriety, obedience, integrity, and respect for the legacy of ancestors. The traditional family was a stable and dependable social institution, which contributed malleable, obedient citizens for a government based on the same Confucian virtues. Has that malleability played a role in the success of a communist government's shaping of a socialist society? In any case, the days of the traditional family appear to be gone forever.

Who Liberated Women?

How has the change to the modern nuclear family come about? As noted earlier, the key lies in the changes in women's and men's roles to accommodate the "liberation" of women. And, much as Western imperialism is to be condemned for its exploitation of China, it must be acknowledged that the seeds for women's liberation were planted during that period. A window to the outside world was opened to give Chinese women a glimpse of feminist activities and opportunities, which lighted a spark of hope for a change in their own restricted existence.

Thanks are due to women missionaries who modeled a less dependent life-style and to Christian missions whose schools offered the first possibility of education for girls. Prior to that time China offered a few schools for boys;

young boys from well-to-do families were educated by tutors in their own homes along with their cousins and brothers. It was improper to educate a girl, even if it was thought she had the capacity to learn. A few indulgent fathers allowed their daughters to learn to read along with their training in fancy embroidery and other household arts. But this was a well-guarded secret lest it spoil her chances of making a good marriage. The first girls who went to mission schools often went against their parents' wishes, risking estrangement from family and community, sometimes ending up as charges of the mission because they had nowhere else to go.

Likewise, foreign industries offered opportunities for factory work to females. They are not to be praised for the degrading sweatshop conditions in which women worked. But earning money of their own, even though it was but pennies a day, was a way out of intolerable home conditions for those rebels who were brave enough to venture it.

Those were the opening wedges which were seized by the most daring Chinese women and girls; it was a small beginning which grew into an organized movement for women's rights. I wonder whether those dedicated Christian missionaries, themselves unliberated by today's standards, realized the Pandora's box they were opening and the effects it would have on the well-disciplined Chinese family! Women, tasting the heady wine of education and economic independence, were reluctant to remain submissive to tyrannical fathers or detested husbands. Some were even prepared to reject marriage and family ties altogether.

They were quick to find other opportunities to show their new freedom. This movement out of the confines of the home was accelerated by the nationalist revolutions of the early part of the century followed by the Japanese War and the civil war. Chinese women noticed that war and heroism are highly valued in a male-dominated society. Therefore, to prove that their worth and their capabilities were equal to those of men, they enthusiastically joined the revolutionary effort. At first they participated by taking over the farm work and encouraging enlistment of their husbands or fathers. They formed work units or hospital corps to serve behind the lines. They participated in publicity teams and social work in combat areas. A few, disguised as men, joined the guerrilla fighting. Some actually organized all-female combat units which were part of the revolutionary army. They thought they were fighting not only in defense of their country but also in defense of women's interests and for a new society which would grant them equal status and opportunity.

Many died as martyrs to the cause and were acclaimed as heroes. They were praised by the leaders, who made flattering speeches about their invaluable assistance, without which the revolution could not have succeeded. But they quickly learned that the glories of battle soon fade and victory on the battlefield does not carry over to victory by the hearthside. When the fighting died down, there was no major change in their domestic situation. But there was demand for everyone's labor to build the new republic. The new government declared the equality of men and women in all spheres of life. It encouraged their participation in jobs outside the home. The serious economic collapse which China had suffered necessitated the contributions of all in order to provide the bare essentials of life. Aside from enhancing the economic situation of their households, women's "productive labor" in building socialism became a means of consciousness raising. Women became aware of their own value and their competence as productive members of the new society which was expected to bring in a new era of freedom and prosperity.

Revolutionary Laws for the New Nuclear Family

While some, both men and women, may have mourned the passing of the old regime and its definition of roles within the familiar traditional family, apparently most were ready for the revolutionary change in another aspect of their living patterns. Much credit is given to the marriage laws of 1950 for spelling out the new expectations and reordering the way of life of a nation.

The enactment of these laws was one of the first accomplishments of the new government. I would think this was one of the most revolutionary things they had done during the entire half century of revolutions! In the first constitution adopted in 1953, there was an equal rights clause. I quote article 53 of the current constitution:

> Women enjoy equal rights with men in all spheres of political, economic, cultural, social, and family life.
> Men and women enjoy equal pay for equal work.
> Men and women shall marry of their own free will. The state protects marriage, the family, and the mother and child.
> The state advocates and encourages family planning.

This prescription is quite a contrast to the traditional family of imperial days. But the marriage laws of 1950 had already spelled out more specifically the duties and responsibilities of both wives and husbands. They give us a picture of today's new family.

With the redistribution of large landholdings, the confiscation of upper-class estates, and the joining of rural families in collectively owned farm communes, the old extended-family pattern gave way to the nuclear family of husband, wife, and their children. A grandparent or other relative may still be included for the sake of housing economy or child care arrangements. Given this new grouping, what changes were prescribed by the new laws?

Arranged marriages were officially prohibited by the stipulation that "marriage is based on the complete willingness of the two parties. Neither party shall use compulsion and no third party is allowed to interfere." In other words, no parental control and no seeking the services of a go-between. At our college in Chengdu there was much talk among the young people about their freedom to choose their own mates without the approval of parents. They were quite elated at the prospects of making a love match. However, we are told that in some remote villages young peasants sometimes seek the help of parents in arranging their marriages or "agreed-upon matches," in which the young people have the freedom to accept or reject the proposed candidate. But, in general, this freedom of choice is one of the valued provisions of the law.

Joint Partners in Marriage

Husbands and wives both have the right to work, study, and take part in social and political activities. Both have the right to own, use, and dispose of property held in common. Each has the right to inherit from the other. Multiple marriages, child brides, and concubines are prohibited. Widows may not be denied the right to remarry. A wife may keep her own name. Either husband or wife may sue for divorce, but he may not seek a divorce while she is pregnant nor for one year after childbirth. The legal age for marriage was raised to 22 for men and 20 for women. Both husband and wife are responsible for the care and support of any children they may have.

While couples may marry at the legal age, they are encouraged to wait until they are older, 26 to 30, as an aid to population control. Shortage of housing and uncertainty of job assignments also promote later marriages, especially in the cities. Students in college or university are forbidden to marry until after graduation. There are married students in school now because of the backlog of older students held over from the six-year closure of schools during the Cultural Revolution. Even these married students are generally required to live in dormitories on campus.

Divorce rates are very low. Couples are encouraged to work out their problems with the help of relatives or friends, or with their neighborhood political group. Sometimes their "wrong attitudes" will be criticized by their co-workers in an attempt to help them see the error of their ways. Divorce will be granted if these efforts at mediation fail. Even in the case of divorce, both parents are responsible for the support of any children. Custody may be given to either parent, depending on which is more suitable under existing circumstances, but the noncustodial parent must contribute to the living and educational expenses of the children.

After 30 years of the new-style marriages, the marriage laws were revised effective January 1981. Few changes were made, primarily only in the cases of those no longer needed now that the public and young people have been weaned away from the former "feudalistic" ideas about marriage and the role of women in society. Restrictions against child brides and concubines were dropped since multiple wives have long been illegal and monogamy is the accepted practice. The law allowing the remarriage of widows was also dropped as unnecessary now. Although the dowry formerly paid by the bride's family and the gifts from the groom's family negotiated as the bride price have both been outlawed, the revised laws still ban the custom of the bride's family demanding gifts from the groom's family.

The old practice of bride and groom not seeing each other until he lifted the veil from her face in the wedding chamber is definitely relegated to the past, but the impulse for gift giving and receiving is evidently more difficult to root out. Some of the old customs still persist in modified form. Especially among the peasants, the groom is still expected to give betrothal gifts to the bride. Household furnishings or special items such as a sewing machine, bicycle, or TV set may be a condition of the bride's consent to marry. The practice of the bride bringing a dowry to the new household has disappeared because she is now a worker and will be contributing an income. Even on the rural communes her work will earn points equal to those of the men, thus adding to her family's share of the proceeds.

Support from the Social Structures

The new marriage laws have brought about tremendous changes in personal lives and family life-styles in the new China. The socialist society attempts to support and encourage marriage and family stability through the legal guarantees which it provides. Some practical assistance in child rearing and homemaking tasks is also provided. Most workplaces have communal dining halls, where families can obtain prepared food for one or all of their daily meals. They also are expected to furnish nurseries or kindergartens for the care of workers' children at a reasonable fee. Maternity-leave policies are quite generous, and health care is available at minimal charge. A new mother gets 56 days of paid maternity leave, up to 70 days for twins or a difficult birth. On return to work the mother may place her child in the nursery and is allowed breaks from work to nurse the baby.

Even such arrangements may not be adequate for one reason or another. The child care center may be too far from home, or the parents may feel they cannot afford it. Grandparents may be readily available at a lower cost. Parents sometimes deposit children with grandparents, bringing them home only on weekends. Some government day-care centers also provide boarding facilities. Our college in Sichuan had a nursery school which cared for children from 2½ to 4 years of age. But I know of one mother

Most workplaces are expected to provide nurseries or kindergartens for the care of workers' children at a reasonable fee.

who preferred to leave her child with her mother-in-law, bringing him home to her campus apartment only on weekends. Child care is a problem for working parents in the new China, but, in general, suitable facilities are much more readily available than in North America. And here we have fewer grandmothers available and willing to take on another round of child rearing.

At this point, perhaps we should take a look at that end of the age spectrum. What is happening to the old people of China? Both sons and daughters are responsible for the care of aged parents, although there are some old people's homes for those who have no children to provide for them. Retirees receive pensions from their places of work, which are supposed to be 70 to 75 percent of their former salaries. Retirement age is relatively young: 50 for women engaged in manual work, 55 for "mental" workers, 60 for men. Their pensions give them an independence and security, but old people are often welcomed in the homes of their children for their baby-sitting services and household help. Their pension income, if pooled with the family earnings, is also a welcome addition. Even in the limited confines of the small apartment of today, there are remnants of the old extended family, but on a completely different basis. One might say that today's extended family is more like a family collective. With the old-style chivalry toward old age and their new-style pension check, the elderly are enjoying the best of both worlds.

I can't vouch for the adequacy of the pension, but I did experience the respect for age. I had never considered myself old, but in China my gray hair attracted a lot of concern on field trips, in climbing steps or any kind of labor. Chinese staff and friends were constantly asking about the state of my energy and health, occasionally giving a supporting hand. I hardly dared stop to rest lest I cause someone to worry! By the time one has gray hair, one is expected to have acquired some wisdom not readily available to the young and to have earned the right to respect. I have no doubt that the Chinese are shocked, as are other Asians, when they hear that we Americans put our old parents away in "old homes" rather than caring for them as part of our families. I'm afraid our excuse of lack of space would not hold water with the Chinese, who would consider our modest homes palatial.

Not All Problems Eliminated

In China today, women's lot has been vastly improved; children and mothers are protected by legal guarantees, men are more involved in home and child care, marriage is much more a joint undertaking, and old people make their contributions to the family welfare. The Chinese family appears to be in less trouble than the North American family when you consider our divorce rate, crime and juvenile delinquency, mental and emotional disturbances, and other social ills. Nevertheless, China has not solved all of its problems in this respect; some political and economic conditions still pose threats to an ideal family life.

Although the state supports marriage and motherhood, political education may make demands on citizens which strengthen political loyalty at the expense of family solidarity. During periods of class struggle or revolutionary zeal, people were urged to criticize, or report on, even their near kin. This practice naturally results in the weakening of family trust. During the Cultural Revolution, Christian parents feared to teach their faith to their children lest they be reported and punished.

The government policy of job placement often disregards the spouse's assignment and separates families, sometimes by great distances. A young male teacher of our acquaintance has a wife and baby daughter living over 200 kilometers away. She, also a teacher, lives with her mother, who cares for the child. He visits them perhaps every three

An old man flies his kite in Tien An Men Square.

months, allowing hardly adequate time for building a close father-daughter relationship or having any influence on her rearing. Jobs are supposedly assigned on the basis of where the workers' skills are needed at the particular time they enter the job market, and transfers are very difficult to negotiate. Young couples often put off marriage, hoping for assignments more favorable to establishing a home. Many people are hopeful that the current, more moderate government will take steps to correct this situation by allowing freer transfers or more choice in job placement. Some of the old imperial tyrannies have been replaced by the tyranny of cumbersome central planning or bureaucratic administration.

The openness of the new regime to foreign exchanges for study or research is bringing limited opportunity for scientists, teachers, or researchers to gain highly prized advanced training. It would take a very dedicated father or mother to turn down such a once-in-a-lifetime windfall, offered only to a chosen few. Yet, it will mean leaving spouse and even young children behind for a year, or two or three. Such is the sacrifice some families will be called on to make for the technological advancement of their country. Of course, the lucky recipients will feel the experience is for the long-term good of the family as well. But it is not ideal.

The Chinese love children, and it is a joy to see the tender, loving care lavished on the young child almost to the point of permissiveness. But the hard facts of life and geography are clearly saying that China has about reached the saturation point as far as population is concerned. The question of family size must be dealt with, and pressure is brought to bear on young parents to help achieve a viable population—one which can be supported by the resources of the nation.

Is One Enough?

The population increase of 80 percent just since liberation obviously cannot continue if the masses are to improve their living conditions. The government has set the ambitious goal of zero population growth by the year 2000. That is a big order considering the present birthrate. However, when we look at recent achievements, we must concede that they might just make it! In 1969 the birthrate was between 35 and 40 per 1,000. This had been reduced to 12 per 1,000 by 1978, a drastic cut in just nine years. But to reach the projected 5 per 1,000 by 1985 and ZPG by the year 2000 calls for even greater effort.

The family planning program was one of the many things grossly neglected during the Cultural Revolution, but it is now being renewed with vigor. It has been relatively successful in urban areas; the rural people are the holdouts, and the rural people make up at least 80 percent of the total. Free contraception, abortions, and sterilizations are offered. Barefoot doctors (paramedical personnel) are being sent into the countryside in a strong educational campaign. And now, besides these long-tried methods, something new has been added. The campaign for one-child families is backed up with enticing rewards and stringent punishments. The concept of one child per couple calls for a radical change of thinking, especially in the rural areas, where large families have been seen as labor and earning power as well as old-age insurance. With this view embedded in the subconscious for centuries, it's hard to shift one's trust to government pension plans and collective labor for food production.

The young couple who pledges to have only one child is immediately rewarded with an honor certificate and a cash bonus monthly or annually. Free maternal and child health care are provided. The child is guaranteed a tuition-free place in a good kindergarten and other schools. Parents receive preferential treatment in housing and job placement. Grain allocation for the sole child is the same as for an adult, and the family's private plot is enlarged by the equivalent of shares for 1½ persons.

A second child would not receive any of these benefits, but neither would it be subject to penalty. Of course, in that event, the one-child agreement would be canceled. A third child, on the other hand, brings economic penalty in the form of a tax or an income reduction and receives no coupons for rationed food and cloth before the age of 14. In other words, the whole family has to share reduced resources in the event of a third child.

Many young couples are opting for the one-child family and its rewards. Peer pressure is strong for limitation of families to one child, or at most two children, for the benefit of the entire society. However, some psychologists and parents are asking how this policy will affect the children who are raised as such privileged characters, and whether the socialization process without sibling interaction will adversely affect their contribution to a society which has placed great emphasis on unselfishness and serving others. Government officials hope their family planning program will be a solution to a crisis situation which need not be a long-term policy once ZPG has been reached.

Children Are Tenderly Nurtured

In spite of problems, Chinese men and women continue to get married, raise families, and together work at improving their living conditions. Has the new-style family been a success? Are children nurtured? Are morally responsible workers and citizens raised up to do the work of the world? Is there a warm and loving atmosphere in the home to

Government and peers pressure couples to limit their families to one child for the benefit of the entire society.

cushion the harsh realities of life in a developing nation? My impression is that parents and other adults show loving concern for children, that grandparents enjoy rather than resent their essential role as baby-sitters, and that child care workers in nurseries and kindergartens do more than custodial care of their young charges. While I did not see an overabundance of toys compared to that of American children, neither would I say that Chinese children are deprived. Youngsters were enjoying games and books, sports equipment and pictures, sometimes creating their own amusements.

Tiny tots in kindergarten learn numbers and words to give them an early start on that hard-to-come-by education. With their rosy cheeks, black eyes, and smiles, they entertained us by singing and dancing. They sat meekly at their little tables, then rose and parroted a greeting at the teacher's signal, and lined up with prompt obedience in an orderly fashion for their performance on the lawn. Perhaps they are regimented, but that is not bad preparation for life in a society that is bound to be somewhat regimented. In general, the ones we observed in the streets and courtyards of our campus romped and cavorted, played and quarreled, were naughty and nice—just like children all around the world.

It is impossible to judge another culture as seen through the filter of our own cultural expectations. There appeared to be much less togetherness of spouses than we expect. At college functions I rarely saw couples attending together. One couple, both on the English faculty, were always at our Friday evening lectures for the department, but it was a long time before I realized that they were spouses and then only because their small son was sometimes with him and other times with her. On special occasions, at banquets or teas for visiting foreigners and VIP's, only the foreign spouses were included. Perhaps this simply means that the wife is not viewed as an adjunct in her husband's business affairs, and vice versa. Marriage partners seem to function more independently in professional and political affairs and spouses go their own ways, a more common trend in our own society than in former times.

The marriages, while now based on free choice, seemed to be less romantically and emotionally overloaded than ours, and expectations more realistic. One reason for failure in marriages in our society may be the quick decisions based on body chemistry and personality attraction—a love which is expected to overcome all difficulties, meet all physical, affectional, and intellectual needs, while maintaining a daily existence on the dizzying heights of cloud nine. Chinese young people are also looking for love and romance, but they look ahead to the nitty-gritty of daily life and work, seeking partners who will fit into their family backgrounds and their plans for the future. We cannot evaluate the quality of Oriental family life purely by our standards. In the new China the present acculturation retains a thread of the past—the view of marriage and home life from the perspective of the good of society rather than the happiness of the individual exclusively.

The Old Argument—Who Does What?

Yet one more question frequently asked by American women, "Are Chinese women really liberated?" I would have to say yes and no. They have a constitutional guarantee of equal rights; they have their liberal marriage laws. They have access to a great variety of jobs. They must be given equal pay for equal work. Their menfolk do many household tasks. Yet there remain some inequalities.

Women may be seen driving big trucks and buses, serving

as medical doctors and teachers and party administrators, working on road and building construction, and doing all kinds of farm labor. There is no apparent discrimination against their entering any field, and when they do the same job as a man, they must receive the same pay. But they don't end up doing exactly the same work. A woman may be shoveling and mixing cement, but a man will likely be laying the bricks. A woman may be wielding pick and shovel, but a man will be doing the more technically skilled tasks. Female teachers may outnumber male, but the heads of departments are more often men. Women party workers tend to be active on the local and county levels, but few are administrators on the national level. Does it all sound familiar?

As to homemaking chores, it depends on whom you ask. Just as men do, practically all women have jobs outside the home. Men can cook, help with cleaning and laundry, and are often seen shopping for vegetables and meat at the marketplaces or carrying home foods from the communal dining halls. But the women insist that they still have the major responsibility to see that all these things get done.

In my class of young English teachers we sometimes got into discussions on who does what in the home. Invariably the men insisted that they do their fair share of housework, and the women insisted that they do not, all in good-natured argument of course. I certainly would not want to be the referee! I did notice that child care especially is considered to be in the realm of women's work. Chinese men use that old argument that women are just naturally endowed with the nurturing gifts. Motherhood is idealized and put on a pedestal. However, one sees many fathers proudly pushing baby carriages and tending little tots. The whole matter of men's and women's roles is a great topic for repeated discussion, but, in the end, one doesn't detect much change in attitude or opinion. What would you say if the Chinese asked you whether American women are really liberated? Men and women on both continents are still working at it. Chairman Mao Zedong once said, "Women hold up half the Heavens." The assumption is that men are holding up the other half.

Hope for Tomorrow

Meanwhile, Chinese parents cherish their sons and daughters and strive to attain for them the best that life has to offer. The dramatic improvements in the lives of millions of people in the last 30 years have been a source of constantly rising expectations. Whether these desires can be realized by modern technology and consumer goods, whether the Chinese can achieve a higher living standard without at the same time falling prey to the social problems which plague highly developed countries, remains to be seen. Love of family motivates much of that aspiration for a more meaningful existence and more satisfying human development. Parents of today hope that their sacrifices and struggle will result in a tomorrow of love, stability, justice, and peace. The quality of life in the homes of the new China will be a determining factor in the quality of life in that dawning tomorrow. We hope those bright-eyed cherubs will be prepared for that brave new world which they are anticipating.

8
To Each According to His Work

My understanding of the Marxist principle of production and distribution—"from each according to his ability; to each according to his need"—was due for a jolt. Repeatedly we heard the slogan "to each according to his work." This was the rationale for wage policies and for experiments in the use of incentives and material rewards. Actually, it is a statement in the constitution. Increased production is being promoted by bonuses, overtime pay, and weighting of work points. But at the same time, it is meticulously pointed out that a very important socialist motivation is still the desire to "serve the people."

Our few lectures on the Chinese economy and briefings by factory and commune managers didn't give us the final word on the workings of the economic system and the state of its health. We did not become experts, but we did pick up some knowledge of the achievements and frustrations since the revolution and some impressions of current trends. My expertise, if any, as an economist is limited to that of a home economist. I am interested, of course, in how people live and work and provide the necessities of daily life. In this area, as in so many others, changes are occurring at such speed as to invalidate already some things which were apparently true in 1981!

Work Is Honorable

The Chinese communists have always respected the dignity of labor and proclaimed the duty of every citizen to contribute productively to the building of the socialist society. The constitution declares that the national economic policy adheres to "the principle of building our country independently, with the initiative in our own hands and through self-reliance, hard struggle, diligence and thrift." This focus is seen as insurance against reversion to the dependency and exploitation of prerevolutionary days. An interesting point on the matter of work as an honorable duty is that the state employs the principle, "He who does not work, neither shall he eat" (PRC constitution, article 10). That has a strangely familiar ring, doesn't it?

How can we reconcile such slogans with our concepts of utopian socialism? A noted Chinese economist, Xue Muqiao, explains that his society is socialist, not communist. Communism is the ultimate goal, which can only be reached in "step-by-step" revolutionary stages. Socialism is the lower phase of communism, an immature stage. Hence, "to each according to his work" is an interim policy until the complete achievement of communism, which operates on the principle of "to each according to his need." Socialism, he says, is the necessary stage between capitalism and communism; during this period of transition it would be wrong to expect all people to be mature enough for a truly egalitarian situation.

Tremendous Task of Rebuilding

When the People's Republic was established in 1949, its citizens had gone through decades of extremely difficult years. Historically, their agricultural economy had always been at bare-subsistence level, subject to the caprice of floods and droughts, sometimes harsh landlords and corrupt officials. Problems were further aggravated by the foreign trade policies, which attracted many rural folks to the cities and accented the differences between rural and urban wealth. As in so many Third World countries, extreme luxury existed beside extreme poverty. The long years of war had left the country's basic facilities shattered and the economy in a shambles. Inflation was unbelievable! Our lecturer on China's economy, to show the gigantic proportions of inflation, listed items which a 100-yuan note would buy between 1937 and 1949. Starting with the purchasing power of two cows in 1937, it shrank to one pig in 1939, 500 grams of flour in 1941, one chicken in 1943, two eggs in 1945, and such an infinitesimal amount of milk by 1949 that I couldn't comprehend the fraction. Perhaps you have heard missionaries tell of having to carry their money in suitcases because of the great bulk required for any purchase. The degradation of the poor in such conditions would be indescribable.

The new country was faced with the gigantic tasks of emergency short-term reconstruction as well as long-term development. The agricultural and industrial economy needed to be restored and cities changed from pockets of consumption to centers of production, to contribute to the economy rather than to be a drain. Land reform was of immediate concern. Living standards of peasants as well as workers needed to be raised. Would the leaders who had successfully waged revolution be able to cope with the problems of peace, the almost insurmountable task of reconstruction? The Chinese are keen on doing things "step-by-step," and those first steps must have appeared to be giant steps. The goal was not just the restoration of a previously viable economy but the structuring of a whole new system.

The leadership was committed to building a socialist society in which private property would be replaced by public ownership of the means of production, and the profit motive replaced by planning in order to control production. The

A rural woman with her large basket and carrying pole.

Chinese system recognized two basic types of ownership of the means of production, which they refer to as "socialist ownership by the whole people" and "socialist collective ownership by the working people." The former refers to ownership by society as a whole, that is, by the state; the latter is the joint ownership by the working people forming a collective. Farmland is predominantly collectively owned although there are some state-owned farms. Industry is predominantly state-owned, with an increasing number of collectives being formed in recent years. A third system, individual ownership, is permitted under certain conditions and with stipulated limitations. This type is now receiving more favorable attention. While all three forms are protected by the state, the first two are considered basic and the third subsidiary.

The first years were concentrated on land reform and the building of small-scale cooperatives for producing and marketing goods needed to improve the well-being and morale of the masses of China's people who had been the backbone of the revolution. Capitalist enterprises were "step-by-step" brought under the supervision and control of the state sector. A conscious effort was made to locate new industries in the interior, in cities which had not been developed by foreign capitalists. To accomplish all this, China signed agreements with the USSR for aid in building factories, as well as rebuilding railroads, ports, and mines.

Soviet Help Available

With the early help of Soviet advisors in establishing and building up the Chinese Communist Party and then aid in reconstruction, it is not surprising that China's first five-year plan (1953-57) resembled the Russian model. The emphasis was on heavy industry, food production on large state-owned farms, strict central control, and the concentration of resources in urban areas. By the end of this five-year period it became clear to the Chinese that the Soviet model was not for them. Urban development placed too great a strain on agricultural production with no compensating rise in the peasants' living standard. Central planning as practiced by the Soviets did not allow the Chinese people their desired participation in decision-making. The Soviet revolution had been backed by workers (factory employees), but the Chinese revolution had as its base the millions of small farmers, the peasants. The political strength of the party depended upon retaining the loyalty of the peasants, and the planning needed to reflect consideration for their welfare. Industrial workers were, and still are, a much smaller segment of society than the tillers of the soil.

Then the Great Leap

By 1957 the Chinese had become disenchanted with this model and these priorities. (Perhaps the Russians had also become disenchanted with the CCP.) Over the next few years Soviet aid was withdrawn, and China had embarked on one of Chairman Mao's major failures, the Great Leap Forward. You will recall that at the inauguration of the People's Republic, Mao proclaimed that the Chinese people had "stood up." Now he hoped to have them "walking on two legs." This campaign aimed to make full use of all human and natural resources and to accomplish development on both fronts (industry and agriculture) in double-quick time. It would make use of primitive methods as well as modern technology, unskilled labor as well as skilled workers. Industry would be planted in the country as well as in the cities; urban dwellers as well as rural people would grow food. Along with the conventional raw materials, innovative use of any local resource was encouraged. Training would be not only theoretical but also practical. Success would depend not only on the pragmatic approach of the "experts" but on the ideological approach of the zealous "reds."

Central controls were relaxed to foster all kinds of projects—industrial plants in agricultural communes (backyard steel mills), do-it-yourself food production by city dwellers, projects calling for skills which the innovators had not yet acquired. The experiment did allow for initiative, utilization of all possible raw materials, opportunity to try new techniques. But the drawbacks were severe and the results disappointing. Sporadic activity upset central plans, the transport system was overtaxed, projects bogged down for lack of raw materials or expertise, and investment funds were wasted in failed projects. Instead of the hoped-for spur to simultaneous agricultural and industrial growth, it turned out to be one of the most serious setbacks to progress in either. The campaign's unrealistic targets were impossible to meet.

One positive result of the Great Leap was the reassessment of priorities and the decision to make agriculture the foundation of the national economy—with industry, research, and education oriented toward the development of "agriculture first." Whereas the order of priorities had been (as in the USSR) heavy industry, light industry, and agriculture, these would now be completely reversed. Agricultural production to improve the lives of the peasants and light industry to provide the desired consumer goods would support the slower, but planned, development of heavy industry.

It was in the aftermath of the Great Leap failure that a new socioeconomic system came into being in the form of people's communes, a system of collective ownership and joint production. State ownership of farms had proven unproductive. The new arrangement was to provide a more functional administrative unit for the development of both agriculture and light industry, decentralize control, make greater use of local resources, and give more autonomy to the people actually involved in the operation.

The first communes were organized in 1958, but the following years were beset with many problems: the withdrawal of Soviet aid, contradictions in government strategy, and several unusually poor crop years. Although there was little opportunity to test the new approach before the onslaught of the Cultural Revolution, some communes did survive and served as pilot projects to prove that they were effective in improving land, increasing production, raising the morale and income of the peasants. After the fury of the Cultural Revolution abated, the switch to collectives was rapid. Eighty percent of the Chinese people now live in communes. It was with the advent of the commune system that "to each according to his work" became the policy for wages.

What Is a Capitalist Roader?

The new system brought a turn for the better in production and living conditions, but a basic ideological struggle had surfaced in the Great Leap which had not been resolved. How shall I explain the two lines of ideology within the party which continued to vie for domination? "Capitalist roader" was an epithet used to describe people who did not wholeheartedly support the socialist way of life. The victory of the revolutionary forces in 1949 meant the defeat of the capitalist system and the inauguration of the socialist system. Theoretically, there were no more capitalists. But there were still some people who tended to favor economic, political, or social policies which, if uninhibited, would support capitalist interests or a capitalist mentality—individualism, desire for personal gain rather than selfless devotion to the good of the whole community. These people were called capitalist roaders. Those on the capitalist road could be identified by certain traits: they placed high value on personal advancement; they considered mental work superior to physical labor, and they tended to defer to an elite leadership and look down on common people; they put their trust in technology and education more than in patriotic self-reliance and dedicated hard labor; they favored monetary or material incentives as motivation for productivity. I think that is enough to give you the picture. Capitalist roaders followed the "expert" line.

Socialist roaders, on the other hand, continued to struggle against selfishness, elitism, and special privilege. They emphasized participation by the common people, improvement of conditions for all of society, service to others rather than self-advancement, and equal respect for the varied skills and gifts which all members bring to a socialist community. The service motive and the satisfactions of a duty well performed were held up as adequate incentives for productivity. This ideological line was known as "red."

The struggle was between "red" and "expert" as the guiding principle for the development of the nation. Mao, who had unswervingly championed the cause of the masses, supported the "red" line, which basically depended on patriotic devotion to the revolutionary cause. But many party members and even the chairman of the People's Republic, Liu Shaoqi, were accused of being capitalist roaders, who believed their economic problems and industrial backwardness could be overcome only by modern technology and trained experts following the example of

Western countries. Some suspected that even Premier Zhou Enlai was on the side of the "expert" line, but the great respect for him as a diplomat and a team player allowed him to keep his balance and remain in the good graces of the party and Mao. His keen intellect and pragmatism no doubt tempered the more radical stance of Mao in their long years of revolutionary partnership. His death, just eight months before that of Mao, was a great loss to the Chinese people.

The "Greening" of the Revolution

The red versus expert argument became a divisive issue during the Great Leap Forward. It became even more disruptive during the power struggle which ensued, precipitating the Great Proletarian Cultural Revolution initiated and led by Mao himself. Mao claimed it was necessary to level society to its 1949 purity and equality; to eliminate a new elite class of bureaucrats, who were taking special privileges for themselves and their families; to take power from the small group of experts who were doing the planning and managing without consulting the workers; to prevent the growing disparity in incomes that would lead to the rebirth of class differences, which the revolution had been fought to abolish.

This period will probably never be fully understood by the Western world, and much of it is controversial and confused even in the minds of the Chinese. With Mao's blessing, groups of students, organized as "Red Guards," sallied forth to slay the dragons of the "four olds"—old habits, old customs, old ideas, old culture. Mao addressed a rally of more than a million students in Beijing's Tien An Men Square in August of 1966. These young zealots with free passes to travel by rail roamed the country attacking any signs of what they considered bourgeois or elitist or one of

A shoe repairman offers his skill to "serve the people".

the "olds." They took the authority upon themselves to bring about the downfall of many officials, and encouraged struggle and criticism among the masses.

This struggle for the hearts and minds of the people resulted in physical violence, the forming of support groups to back certain government cadres or factory personnel, armed conflict in city streets, and disruption of work in both city and countryside. The nation stood at the brink of economic collapse. Millions of city and educated youth had to go to the country to do manual labor; peasants were placed in schools and jobs for which they were unprepared. Ruling cadres and party officials aligned themselves with factions of the young Red Guards in attempts to protect their positions and influence. Ancient historic sites and valuable art treasures were damaged or destroyed. Factional infighting and violence did untold damage to the nation's physical facilities as well as to the unity of the people. The most violent phase was between 1966 and 1969, but the revolution did not officially come to an end until 1976.

While Mao's rationale for the "greening of the revolution" had some validity, the situation seems to have gotten out of hand and at times bordered on anarchy. The Mao cult, which is now condemned, was propagated by the Red Guards' devotion to Mao's "little red book" and the fervor with which they quoted Mao Thought. Future historians will have to be the final judges of this chaotic period. Right now some Chinese point out values derived from the upheaval—the restoration of a greater degree of equality and the elimination of special privileges for a favored few. Most take a critical view of the devastation and suffering, of which nearly every family had some experience, which set back all sectors of the economy, education, scientific research, and from which the country is still struggling to recover.

Both Needed in the Modern World

After Mao's death and the coming to power of the less radical faction, now called moderates, development policy has officially been the combination of both "red" and "expert." But since the opening to the outside world and the bid for foreign technological aid, it is increasingly coming down on the side of "expert." What is happening now, Mao would have labeled capitalist road or counterrevolutionary, but the new leaders appear to have the support of the great majority of Chinese socialists. If they are to become a fully modernized and industrially developed nation by the year 2000, their stated aim, rapid change is imperative. While truly significant gains have been made in the past 32 years largely by diligent work, independent initiative, struggle, and self-sacrifice, the target for the next 18 years will undoubtedly demand modern technology and even more capitalist-road incentives.

The use of material rewards and individual responsibility as incentives for increasing the quality and quantity of production is definitely the growing pattern now. During the Cultural Revolution everything outside of central planning and state control was looked upon as capitalist. The use of work points—which give added credit for quality work, for more difficult tasks, for tasks requiring special skills, and for overtime work—was repudiated in favor of egalitarianism. All workers were to be treated alike regardless of output. Sideline occupations and individual initiative on private plots were considered to be capitalist efforts for self-advancement.

Against this backdrop the changes in management policy of the past few years are especially striking. The trend now is to give enterprises of all kinds more power in the management of their own affairs, to take into account the factors of supply and demand, to give managers the responsibility of finding raw materials, hiring staff, and finding outlets for the manufactured products. The manager of a large factory in Chengdu told us that his biggest problems are determining what product is most needed, regulating the amount to be placed on the market, acquiring the best and cheapest raw materials, and locating sales outlets. Before, the state set quotas, and every factory was allotted the precise amount of materials, labor, and funds needed to meet the target. Whether the finished product ever got out of stockpiles, was marketable or profitable, was the worry of central planning, not the local manager. That has all changed. Our factory manager recognized that there were elements of competition in the new scheme, but it has increased quality and quantity of output and raised worker morale. He is frankly agreeable to making use of the best of both worlds.

Sichuan Province was a pioneer in the experiment to stimulate local initiative and increase personal responsibility. It was undertaken under the leadership of none other than the current premier of the PRC, Zhao Ziyang, who was earlier party secretary for Sichuan Province. Economist Xue Muqiao in his new book, *China's Socialist Economy*, puts in a plug for the beneficial effects of the new policy. He encourages less control by central planning and more flexibility on the local level to take advantage of marketing and labor conditions. The state, he says, should follow the principle of "strict planning in major affairs and flexibility in minor ones." He wants it clearly understood that this is still good socialist practice. The trouble doesn't lie in the socialist system but in mistakes that have been committed by the bureaucracy in making arbitrary decisions without regarding economic laws and the workers' democratic rights. The pragmatism of the new leadership does not indicate a desire to abandon the socialist economic system but to make it more effective.

Life on a Commune

Since the overwhelming majority of Chinese live on communes, we want to look at that segment of the economy, note the organization and life-style of those millions of people. These cooperative enterprises are organized on three levels: the commune level has overall responsibility for planning and general management of a fairly extensive area; the production brigade has responsibility for certain industries, commercial ventures, or farmlands; the production team is the basic unit in assigning and carrying out specific tasks for any of the projects of the brigade. In spite of variations in statistics I shall try to give you some averages to show the scope of commune operations. There is wide variation in the size of communes depending on the density of population, conditions of soil and terrain, and types of production possible. The average number of people on a commune is said to be 14,700, the average area 5,000 acres. We visited a commune near Chengdu which was composed of 27,000 people in 7,000 households, farming approximately 3,700 acres of land. That one also operates 148 factories as well as numerous sideline industries related to farming. It maintains its own schools through secondary level, a hospital and clinics with 42 doctors and 18 other medical personnel.

Commune headquarters are usually located in one of the larger towns. Commune officials are responsible for the overall management of the entire commune; they relate to government authorities and see that central plans are followed. They may administer 5 to 10 brigades and 50 to 250 production teams. They receive funds from the brigades and teams to carry on projects and services which benefit the entire commune, such as water conservation or irrigation systems. They may invest in and maintain heavy machinery which is to be used by all the component groups but would be too costly for them to own as individual units.

The production brigade, the second level, may supervise only a few, or up to 15 or 20, production teams depending on local conditions and types of projects. The brigade may own some equipment shared by all the teams; oversee irrigation works; operate factories, fish farms, or forestry projects. Usually education and medical care are provided at this level. Brigade leaders communicate production quotas and policies passed down the bureaucratic chain of command. Their headquarters are located in smaller towns.

The production team is the smallest, and probably most important, unit of management. It may consist of from 10 to

The overwhelming majority of Chinese live in communes. On the average, 33 households work 50 acres of land.

100 households. In some cases it constitutes an entire rural village. The average is 33 households working 50 acres of land. The team is the basic accounting unit, assigns daily tasks, keeps records of work points, and pays wages and other obligations. An important difference between commune members and workers in state-owned enterprises is that commune members actually own the property, albeit collectively, and share any profits of their joint labor. Families usually live in their own houses. Team members participate in the decision-making process, although certain state quotas must be met. All members receive allocation of a private plot of ground, which they may use for their own purposes. Up until a few years ago only 5 to 7 percent of the land was set aside for private use, but this has now been raised to 12 to 15 percent of the total. Families use the land for intensive cultivation of vegetables or fruits, or for raising chickens, pigs, and other animals. They use such produce to supplement the family diet or sell it for cash at the local free market. Some engage in sideline occupations such as fishing, hunting, handicrafts, or raising silkworms to produce additional income.

The New Look down on the Farm

To promote greater effort on the part of members, many communes are trying a new technique called the "contract system." A certain enterprise or specified piece of land is contracted to a portion of the work team, a household or even a few individuals, who undertake to carry out the project and meet a certain quota. Any returns above the quota become their private property. For example, a family may be allocated a few acres of land from which they must provide a specified amount of grain in order to meet the team's quota. Whatever they can produce beyond that amount is their own. Contracts may be made to operate sidelines such as forestry, fishing, repair shops, equipment maintenance, or even personal services. One enterprising team member contracted for an abandoned piece of equipment; with his rehabilitated machine he hires out his services to other team members.

This switch to personal incentive has paid off with increased and higher-quality production and greater satisfaction among commune members. In fact, some communes are practicing what they call an "all-round contract" system, which divides up all the land among the households—some good and some bad fields, some far and some near fields—to be cultivated by each household without direct daily supervision of the team leader. The "new" way of farming sounds very much like the old family farm with support and cooperation from relatives and neighbors. They say it is highly successful.

Perhaps you are curious, as I was, about how a communal group disburses its income. A reporter for the magazine *China Reconstructs* (May 1981) recorded the process of one team's 1980 income settlement. The team contained 31 households, with a total of 117 people, of whom 35 were workers. They cultivated jointly 125 acres of farmland. When they shared the year's profits, each member (worker) received a cash amount of 228 yuan ($152) and an average of 200 kilograms of food grain for each person of the team's households. (Production teams acquire cash income from crops sold to the government, for services provided to other teams, or in profits from sideline industries.) The cash income these members received from the team was only 60 percent of their total earnings. The other 40 percent came from their private plots and side activities.

If you were a member of that team, what could you buy

Three workers on a campus take time out for a simple meal.

with your 228 yuan? (Take two-thirds of the amount to figure U.S. dollars.) A bicycle would cost you about 140 yuan, a transistor radio 30 yuan, a wristwatch 70 yuan, cloth 1 yuan per meter (about 39 inches). It would take some careful spending.

At the end of each year the team's accountant must calculate the total output of production, total income of the team, expenditures for the year, work points earned by each member, the cash value of the work points, and the amount of food grain to be distributed. Who gets what from the team income? Members received 69.5 percent, the state received

2 percent as tax, 17 percent went for expenses of the year, and 11.5 percent was put into a contingency fund.

Besides dividing the cash income, the production team must make the annual grain distribution. First they set aside the amount needed to meet the state grain tax, and the amount needed for seed and for animal feed. The remainder is divided among team members. The formula called for 60 percent to be divided among all members (children and old people as well as workers), 40 percent to be divided among the working members according to the work points each had earned. This system ensures a basic amount for all members but an additional amount for the labor contributed by each household—"to each according to his work." A family of five with two full-time workers and one half-time, under this formula received a total of 220 kilos per member. (A kilogram is a little over two pounds in our system.)

There were also special considerations. A family with a son in the army received credit for 500 work points for him and an additional 20 kilos of grain to compensate for the loss of his labor. An 80-year-old woman with no family received 225 kilograms of grain and 50 yuan plus vegetables and fruit. She receives partial support from the brigade, including free medical care, housing, and clothing. Orphans and families of "revolutionary martyrs" also receive special rations.

Peasants and Workers Seek Improved Living

Agriculture holds a place of great importance in the Chinese economy. It is not only the livelihood of more than 80 percent of the population; it also provides 70 percent of the raw materials for light industry and 25 percent of foreign exports. But while agriculture is given priority, there is still a large gap between workers in the industrial and service sectors and those in the agricultural sector. We learned that peasants' per capita income averaged only 83 yuan while overall per capita income averaged 380 yuan. The former figure is for cash income only and does not take into account the farm produce and grain which make up part of the farmer's total income.

There is great disparity in the wealth and income of communes. The ones we visited in Sichuan Province, the garden spot of China, were decidedly better off than those in a mountainous area or an area with less rich soil would be. The government tries to compensate by lowering taxes in poor areas or subsidizing certain projects. In spite of low incomes, purchasing power is growing more rapidly than consumer goods. Peasants are purchasing more consumer goods, such as bicycles, sewing machines, radios, TV sets, and watches. Consumer patterns are also changing in the city. The former order of priorities—food, clothing, and consumer items—has now been reversed. At the same time, consumers are buying better-quality goods. Demands for children's products are on the increase since one-child families have more cash to lavish on that one child. There is still a shortage of such conveniences as washing machines, refrigerators, and electric fans, but statistics tend to manifest an improvement in living standards and the general consumer economy.

Still, there is much room for growth and improvement in industry, and planners hope that the new management policies will stimulate production in this sector as well as in the service sector. Farm-related work engages 75 percent of China's work force. Of the remaining 25 percent who are nonagricultural workers, only 30 percent are industrial employees. Wage statistics are hard to pin down, but the estimated average income for workers in 1978 was $415, with incomes ranging from $186 to $560 depending on the family situation. Wage earners are paid on a wage scale of eight grades. Skilled workers in the top grades make up only 15 percent, semiskilled 45 percent, and unskilled 40 percent of the total work force. While seniority is another factor in these categories, they reflect roughly the technological level of industry and the need for improved educational facilities.

Some Unemployment in Spite of Guarantee

The Chinese constitution guarantees a job for everyone willing and able to work. Working age is considered to be from 15 to 64, and the 1979 figures show that 72 percent of this age-group was in the active labor force. The other 28 percent would include the relatively few full-time housewives and some retirees. For some time it was claimed that no unemployment existed. Now, however, unemployment is acknowledged as a problem. Jobs were found for four million unemployed during the first five years of the PRC, and full employment was maintained up to 1966. Some of the present unemployment ("job-waiting" as they call it) is blamed on the economic collapse caused by the chaotic conditions of the Cultural Revolution decade. Many factories ceased operation. The ultraleftists in power supposedly sent 13 million school graduates to work in the countryside and a smaller number of country youth were assigned to the cities. After the revolution the former filtered back to the cities and the latter stayed on, swelling the urban populations beyond the cities' capacities to provide for their residents.

Too much emphasis was again placed on heavy industry, which provides fewer jobs. According to the head of China's State Labor Bureau, capital investment of one million yuan creates only 94 jobs in heavy industry compared to 257 jobs in light industry and even more in the service trades. The leftist fear of individual enterprise abolished the individual economy—self-employed tradespeople or independent collectives, which in 1966 still gave employment to two million people. Also, the excessive population growth encouraged by the political climate of those years is now beginning to show up in the labor market.

High unemployment has liberalized the policy regarding private and collective initiative. In fact, they are being encouraged to absorb the jobless youth in many cities. Beijing claims to be using the skills of a half million young people in small cooperative sales and service enterprises which the state has not been able to offer. They range from tea stalls and snack shops to bicycle and radio repair shops to dry cleaning and tailor services to photo and handicrafts shops. Many have been started with loans from neighborhood political committees or the pooling of individual resources. These flourishing businesses provide opportunity for unemployed young people and raise the morale of the entire community, according to enthusiastic news reports. They operate under state licensing but with freedom to innovate and experiment—exploiting the profit motive while providing "service to the people."

New management policies may shatter the "iron rice bowl" in the end. We heard much criticism of the policy which ensured a job to a worker regardless of his performance. This policy of retaining all employees even when they do shoddy work or fail to do their share of communal work is known as the "iron rice bowl," perhaps an occupational hazard of any bureaucracy, whether socialist or capitalist. The iron rice bowl is being threatened with something less durable. Will it be "tenure according to his work"?

The Chinese make a distinction between capitalist unem-

Customers choose their favorite cuts of meat from this open-air stall.

ployment and socialist "job-waiting." They say their unemployed are primarily new entrants into the job market—middle-school graduates who can't go to college, those out of the job market because of ill health or some (perhaps family) obligation, and youth returning from service in the countryside. Heads of families are employed and can help sons and daughters who are waiting for job assignments. Sometimes an obliging father is willing to retire a bit early in order to let his son have the job. It is said that workers displaced by technology will not be abandoned but assigned to other work, not (as economist Xue says) "set adrift, destitute and homeless as in a capitalist society." Today unemployment is a worldwide problem even in labor-intensive economies. Leaders of socialist countries may find it as difficult to fulfill the guaranteed right to work, as leaders of capitalist countries find it difficult to carry out campaign promises to improve the economy.

Where There's Life There's Change

In the 1980's, change is the hallmark of China. What the many changes of the past three years will bring is anyone's guess. We were impressed by the openness with which people discussed the mistakes of the past, with the new candor on the part of government bureaus in releasing statistics which were formerly undisclosed. We were, however, struck by the way in which many statistics cited by our lecturers on production increases, living improvements, and other signs of hope harked back to the "smashing on the Gang of Four."

Following the death of Chairman Mao and the official end of the Cultural Revolution in 1976, Madam Mao and three ultraleft collaborators were arrested and charged with many of the crimes of that period and a conspiracy to take over the government when Mao had departed from the scene. But I don't remember ever hearing it calmly stated that Madam Mao and her associates were arrested and charged. It was always the "smashing of the Gang of Four"—with emphasis! They served as a handy scapegoat for all the economic, educational, and social ills of those disastrous years. After their "smashing," things immediately had taken a turn for the better. Everyone was saying, "It could never happen again." And everyone seemed optimistic that the dawn of a new and better era was at hand.

Since 1978 the emphasis is on achieving the Four Modernizations by the year 2000. In short, this plan visualizes a China fully modernized, independent, prosperous, and progressive by the end of this century. Remarkable achievements have been made against great odds in the past 30 years. Who is to say that these extremely optimistic goals cannot be achieved in the next 20 years? Above some critical voices and some sincere doubts about the road ahead, a general atmosphere of confidence and determination prevails. Major elements of the dream are the high hopes pinned on modern technology and the great expectations from the sudden new friendship with the United States. Western influences are already surfacing among the urban and educated Chinese. Personally, I hope they will not precipitously abandon some of the admirable and sound values which undergird their simple revolutionary life-style, nor completely give up their respect for labor and the joy of serving the people.

Our Day on a Commune

Our experience as workers on a commune in the PRC turned out to be something of a fantasy. Not that we didn't work! Picking oranges from conveniently small trees for about an hour was an enjoyable lark. Digging taro (a starchy edible root) and sweet potatoes in heavy clay soil, however, did use some muscles of which we tenderfoot peasants hadn't been consciously aware before. But I'm sure the red tape of fulfilling the request for our group to have this "work experience" on a commune, the ritual of tea and briefing by the commune manager, the elaborate feast prepared for us in a commune restaurant, the long rest period and tea break, the time lost by commune members in supervising and facilitating our labor (perhaps even repairing any damages we did) more than offset any positive results of our workday.

It was an interesting day for us, and the peasants seemed to enjoy watching our enthusiastic, if unskilled, efforts. (What did they expect from capitalist "intellectuals"?) We did have the joy of "serving the people." We did have opportunity to visit some peasant homes. We went back to the Panda Palace laden with bags of oranges for our personal consumption and sweet potatoes for communal consumption in our dining hall. I leave it to you to decide who benefited more, the helpers or the helped. There is the further question of whether the policy "to each according to his work" might have been violated on that workday.

9
Seeing the Sights of China

We cannot leave China without a quick armchair sightseeing tour. It would take years to explore all the natural beauties and varied landscapes, the ancient cultural treasures and the sites of historical significance. We'll just take a drive around the city and through the countryside, visit only a few of the tourist attractions, to give us a bird's-eye view of what China has to offer her visitors.

City Traffic

We've already noted the scarcity of autos and the great abundance of bicycles. This fact should not lead us to expect a simple traffic pattern downtown or on the highways. Many other types of vehicles of all speeds clutter up the traffic lanes. There are the motor-powered ones such as trucks, buses, tractors, army-green jeeps, and heavy construction equipment. There are the few animal-powered ones drawn by oxen or small horses. There are the human-powered ones, pulled by bicycle or pushed or pulled by hand.

Unbelievable loads can be carried on bicycle racks, from enormous baskets of vegetables to trussed porkers on the way to be slaughtered to a standing child safely strapped to a pedaling parent. I actually saw full-size sofas being delivered by bicycle. Low-slung two-wheel carts pushed or pulled by one to four persons transport muscle-straining loads of brick, rocks, coal cakes, or foodstuffs. Men, women, or mixed teams may supply the person power. That old standby, the carrying pole, finds many uses on the city streets. A simple pole across the shoulder with basket or bucket suspended from each end balances the load of a fruit vendor, the farm produce of a peasant, or the tools of a tradesman.

The synchronizing of all these wheels and legs moving at varying speeds requires some artful maneuvering. The traffic policeman on his umbrella-sheltered little round drum at the center of an intersection does his best to keep things moving, but bike riders and pedestrians need to be alert. Street scenes in a city like Chengdu can be fascinating. Much of the business of life takes to the open air. The entire fronts of small shops open directly to the passersby. Vegetable and fruit stands do a brisk business at curbside. Tailors move their sewing machines out into the sunshine. Clothing, books, and consumer items are displayed on the sidewalk, reminiscent of the end-of-season "sidewalk days" in American towns and cities. At the same time, residents of the area are performing household tasks by their doorsteps, adding to the air of a lively, generally good-natured scramble of daily chores and business pursuits of an energetic people.

Countryside Scenes

As we drive through the countryside, the swarms of people and activity are less hectic, but it rarely happens that we are not within sight of human beings in such densely populated areas as Sichuan Province. There is, however, a restful air about the neatly laid-out fields traced by the raised banks of the irrigation ditches. Even when the field has a work team of 15 to 20 people spread across its rich soil cooperatively hoeing, weeding, or transplanting, there is a certain calm in their rhythmic, methodical movements.

A common sight is a team of workers with long-handled wooden dippers applying the liquified fertilizer from large buckets to the crop rows. This precious fertilizer comes from the "night soil"—human excrement—carefully collected for this purpose. The wooden elongated barrel-shaped container on wheels, sometimes called the "honey wagon," makes its rounds in all communities. Organic fertilizer from animals is insufficient for the demanded intensive crop production. Commercial fertilizer is scarce and expensive. At the public health risk of spreading diseases, most Asian countries use human fertilizer. That is one reason they do not eat uncooked vegetables as freely as we do.

I was struck by the careful stewardship of the soil. Every available inch seems to be lovingly encouraged to produce something edible. Some institutions may enjoy green lawns, and parks may grow grass, but the average householder grows a useful crop right up to the foundations of the house. Roadside berms, banks of streams, even irrigation ditches do double or triple duty. The earthen walls of irrigation ditches may have green vegetable seedlings transplanted on their sloping sides, their rounded tops a mound for sweet potatoes unless needed for a footpath. In some areas the green fields are outlined by mulberry trees growing from the irrigation ditch walls. Their leaves will feed the silkworms, which are an important enterprise in China.

The small fields in strips, squares, or odd shapes look immaculately tended and weed free. An old-fashioned wooden plow guided by a man or woman and pulled by a water buffalo is not an unusual sight. The small tractors with their grasshopperlike appearance, exposed innards and long handlebars, polluting the atmosphere with noise and smoke, are common to both city and farm. Occasionally, one sees a field large enough to warrant a regular tractor, more familiar to our eyes. Of course, on the narrow mountain terraces the soil must be turned over clod by clod with a sturdy, broad hoe. At unbelievable heights such terraces look as if they might hold but a single row of corn. The crop has been harvested, but the still-standing dry stalks give a faint golden wash to the hillsides. One wonders how far the farmer must commute to those fields.

The rural scene is enjoyable through the windows of a bus or train, and mountain roads give fantastic views. But life is not easy in rural China, especially in the remote areas. Farm homes often look rather dark and dreary. Men, women, and children all work very hard. In spite of life's demands they generally look cheerful and well fed. Life has improved; they await easier days ahead.

The Storehouse of Heaven

In the many field trips from our base at Chengdu, we had opportunity to enjoy the Sichuan countryside. Chengdu boasts a history of more than 2,200 years, was formerly called The Storehouse of Heaven, and has long been famous for its many crafts—embroidery, lacquer ware, silver artistry, pottery, bamboo ware, cutlery, silk weaving, jade and ivory carving. It became known as the City of Brocade 2,000 years ago and still makes the traditional brocade and woven silk in its many textile factories. In visits to some of these factories we saw artisans at work carving intricate and elaborate objects of ivory and jade, designing precious silver articles, weaving bamboo into useful and beautiful pieces, embroidering delicate sheer silk with elegant designs perfect to the view from both sides of the fabric. Luxurious handwoven wool rugs are still painstakingly produced for export to affluent customers in the Western world.

Patience, skill, and years of training are required, not to mention a steady hand and sharp eyes. These workshops are nowadays a part of the tourist circuit, and their products supply some of the foreign exchange as China reaches out to the wider world. Many of the handicrafts will find their way to the shelves of North American stores.

Tourist Attractions from the Past

We can't begin to cover all the tourist attractions, but we should look at some of the most famous ones of which you have heard. If you were to go to Beijing, the capital city for many centuries, you would want to see the elaborate complex of buildings which made up the Imperial Palace of the Ming and the Qing emperors. Built between 1406 and 1420, they are said to be the finest example of ancient Chinese architecture and the most complete group of ancient buildings to survive to the present time. Palace buildings containing more than 9,000 rooms, set in a 250-acre park, were occupied for 500 years by emperors' families and courts. The compound is known as the Forbidden City; entry by foreigners or common citizens was strictly not allowed. The grounds are surrounded by a 35-foot-high wall as well as a wide moat. Within these confines, emperors and their favorites lived lives of idleness and extravagance. The tyrannical Empress Dowager, the last of the rulers, is said to have had more than 100 dishes at each meal—enough for a day's food for 5,000 peasants. That figure seems impossible; perhaps it included the value of the gold, silver, and jade dishes from which she ate!

The Forbidden City is now a public museum, open to the people and toured by many visitors. Its buildings with their typically Chinese upturned roof corners are restored to their

A sculpture of revolutionary heroes in Tien An Men Square.

original gleaming colors, predominantly red with decorations of brilliant blues, greens, and gold. They are known by such intriguing names as Hall of Supreme Harmony, Hall of Perfect Harmony, Palace of Heavenly Purity, Palace of Earthly Tranquillity.

Entrance to the palace grounds is through the Gate of Heavenly Peace (Tien An Men). It was at this central gate that the immense portrait of Mao Zedong always hung in pictures we saw of Tien An Men Square. The grandstands below seat 20,000 officials and guests to review parades or hear speeches. The square, the largest public square in the world since being enlarged in 1958 to 98 acres, can hold a million people. It has been the site of mass rallies, demonstrations, parades, and celebrations. A guidebook points out that the Forbidden City typifies the "closed-in" past of China, while Tien An Men Square typifies the "open" future. This flagstone-paved square in the center of modern Beijing is one of its most impressive sights and is surrounded by imposing landmarks of the People's Republic.

On its north side is the ancient Gate of Heavenly Peace, which leads to the old imperial palaces, now a public park. On the east are the National Museums of Chinese History and of the Chinese Revolution. On the west is the Great Hall of the People, where the National People's Congress convenes, with meeting space for 10,000 people plus other conference rooms. Richard Nixon was honored here in 1972 by a dinner for 5,000 guests. On the south is the Memorial Hall to Mao Zedong, the mausoleum housing his remains, which was completed on September 9, 1977, the first anniversary of his death. In the center of the square is the Monument to the People's Heroes, an impressive obelisk reaching 36 meters (118 feet) to the sky and standing on a base carved with a series of panels depicting soldiers, peasants, and workers in revolutionary scenes. The obelisk bears inscriptions in the calligraphy (handwriting) of Chairman Mao Zedong and Premier Zhou Enlai. The entire Square of Heavenly Peace (Tien An Men) is a place of great significance to Chinese national pride and patriotic loyalty.

I liked the quiet simplicity and beautiful lines of the Temple of Heaven, which was built in 1420 in a large park near Beijing as the private worship place for Ming and Qing emperors. Here they offered sacrifices and prayed for good harvests and heaven's blessings on their endeavors. The three-tiered round building on a three-tiered marble terrace has a triple cone-shaped roof of blue tiles supported by a wooden frame and columns, which in the center reach a height of 60 feet. It was constructed without the use of a single nail. Guidebooks claim its 15th-century builders used the most advanced principles of architecture, mechanics, and geometry. The famous Echo Wall surrounding the courtyard has such good acoustics that persons standing at opposite ends and speaking in normal tones near the wall can easily hear each other. There is also the acoustical phenomenon of the Three Echoing Stones; a hand clap from the first stepping-stone produces a single echo, from the second stone a double echo, and from the third a triple echo. The effect is produced by the carefully measured distances from the wall. It is a curiosity which every tourist wants to test. Perhaps it detracts attention from the fullest appreciation of the aesthetic Temple of Heaven, but it reminds us of the innovative talents of the ancient engineers.

More Sights Outside Beijing

Even people who live in gilded palaces like to get away from it all. So we have the Summer Palace of the rulers on a 700-acre park on the shores of Lake Kunming just seven miles from the city. Its major building, White Cloud Palace on the top of Longevity Hill, was built by the emperor in 1791 as a tribute to his 60-year-old mother. (Was there some connection between the age of 60 and the name "Longevity"?) She was still active enough to enjoy the out-of-doors. The Painted Gallery, a covered walkway of 2,388 feet, was built along the lake (that's nearly a half mile!). Its brilliantly and intricately patterned ceiling and railing add a touch of man-made beauty to a stroll here. She also ordered the carving of a marble boat, which sits "anchored" in the lake, no doubt a comfortable place to catch the breezes without the danger of motion sickness. History tells us that funds for this project were diverted from their intended use of improving the navy. Whatever the state of the empress mother's health, I venture to guess that she rarely climbed the many flights of steps to the palace at the top of Longevity Hill. It was a long climb, and many modern 60-year-old women could be found perched on a step for a much needed breather! It is a lovely setting for this beautiful filial act of kindness by the emperor. However, that it is now a park open to the people is even more beautiful.

Before leaving Beijing area we'll want to take an excursion of about 40 miles to the Great Wall. We're already familiar with its history and purpose. Remnants of the old Ten Thousand Li Wall (almost 4,000 miles) remain as a historical monument and tourist attraction. The wall has been the only man-made object visible to astronauts in their orbit of the earth. The amount of brick and stone used in its construction could build an eight-foot dike around the earth. As you climb the steep incline at spots, you can imagine the six-span horse team running side by side on its wide roadway, the

Canadians Susan Weber and Mary Ette Kramer from Goshen College, Goshen, Indiana, enjoy their visit to the Great Wall of China.

The Avenue of the Animals, leading to the Ming tombs.

sentries keeping watch from the blockhouses or towers at strategic points. But most enjoyable is the view of the rolling green hills extending as far as the eye can see.

On the way back to the city we take a side trip to the site of the Ming tombs in a beautiful valley surrounded by mountains. Again we traverse ground which was formerly forbidden to the common people. We go past the 30-foot-high stone turtle, up the Avenue of the Animals guarded by stone statues of giant animals alternately standing and kneeling, then past the stone statues of 12 imperial ministers. This site was constructed in the late 16th century, and 13 Ming emperors are buried here. Two of the tombs have been excavated, displaying huge underground palaces. Only the sepulchre of Ding Ling, buried in 1620 with two wives, has been opened. His marble vault four stories underground yielded magnificent treasures, which are now housed in a museum. The others are still resting undisturbed in their chilly underground palatial vaults, surrounded by their useless earthly treasures.

We Must See Mount Emei

Just for fun I'd like to take you along on one of the most exciting tours of our China sojourn. National Day in China is October 1, and citizens have a two-day holiday to celebrate the founding of the PRC in 1949. Sichuan Teachers' College officials generously offered our group a three-day trip to Mount Emei, a popular resort which is a long day's bus ride from Chengdu, including a rest stop, midday meal, and a side excursion to see the Giant Buddha of Leshan.

Travelers on China's highways have some trouble finding a public rest room, and our Chinese staff had to make suitable arrangements for the comfort of their foreign guests on long trips. One such welcome stop was at Leshan; we were taken through an industrial-type courtyard to some humble dwellings where kind hosts allowed us to use their outside facilities, which were combined with a pig shed. The extremely fat hogs taking their ease in the other half of the shanty seemed not at all disturbed by the foreign invasion.

Meals can also pose some problems, but our diligent staff had made prearrangements at a local restaurant. The meal that day was memorable because we were allowed to eat with the other patrons rather than to be secluded behind a screen or other buffer from the Chinese diners. We were seated at the usual round tables, where we could all reach the serving dishes with our chopsticks. An excited kitchen staff brought us our filled rice bowls, and we proceeded to eat in the same general fashion as everyone around us. We could not get by, however, without the usual fanfare. The restaurant probably had a record crowd that day as passersby came in to watch the foreigners eat. And as we left, the vendors who had congregated around the entryway were prepared to sell us their fresh fruit and other goodies. Our group, sometimes the typical American tourists when it came to shopping, stocked up for the remainder of the long ride.

Detour to the Giant Buddha

With some trepidation (on my part) we boarded the riverboat which would take us to view the Giant Buddha from the middle of the river. College officials had repeatedly warned us to tell our students that they must be very cautious and follow instructions, so I feared some unseen danger lurking out there. In retrospect I realize it was their usual concern for our safety and the success of the exchange program. Our excursion was not entirely by water; we got some exercise as we climbed the hill behind this immense statue to get a closer view of his features. Carved in mountainside rock and overlooking a well-traveled river, the Buddha sits 71 meters (233 feet) high; it took 90 years to carve. Originally built to ensure the safety of sailors at this accident-prone spot, he has watched over the river traffic for more than a thousand years. Modern Chinese question whether safer boat travel is due to his presence or to some later-day dredging. We climbed over the hills to see several pagodas, then made our way back to the highway and our waiting bus.

Speaking of Buddhas, this one was the largest but not the only one we visited in China. We must have seen thousands on our various outings. At one place there were 500 Buddha statues on display with no two alike. Their expressions ranged from the benign (angelic) to the malevolent (almost) demonic)—compassionate, philosophic, cheerful, comic, stern, sad, serious, noncomittal. Name it and they had it. Guests were told that they might determine their own personality type by counting the Buddhas. When you reached the number of your age, that Buddha would reveal your type. An interesting pastime in that maze of Buddhas, but I've already forgotten which one was typical of me!

Toward evening we finally arrived at our destination in the shadow of the famous and popular Mount Emei. It was at this very place that Generalissimo Chiang Kai-shek had his summer headquarters—a lovely spot for rest and relaxation even in those days. The spot is now a vacation area for "the people." Our students were housed in hostels as were the other prospective mountain climbers. Atlee and I had a room in one of several VIP lodges with all the old-style accoutrements, including our own bathroom. We all took our simple camp-style meals at the dining hall along with many Chinese and some Japanese tourists who were also making the climb. My only memory of the food is that the rice was set out in huge wooden tubs, from which we filled our own rice bowls as often as we liked. Mountain climbers eat heartily.

Mysterious Mountain

Every red-blooded Chinese likes to climb to the top of Mount Emei—the Golden Summit more than 10,000 feet high. The mountain itself is shrouded in the ever hanging cloud of fog. But at the Golden Summit one stands above the fog and gets a beautiful view, especially in early morning when mountaintops are bathed in the radiance of the rising sun. Late in the afternoon the viewer may see the Magic Light, which appears as a multicolored ring of light in the sky with the shadow of the viewer in the middle of the ring. The ring follows the shadow as the viewer moves. Mount

Emei had been in earlier centuries one of the Buddhist sacred places, and this light phenomenon was known as the Emei Buddhist Glory. Modern-day scientists and tourists refer to it as the Magic Light.

The mountains are still dotted with Buddhist monasteries, some of them catering to the needs of tourists on their way to the peak. Those of our accompanying Chinese staff who had made the trip to the top thought it was a pity we would miss this wonderful sight. Because of our limit to one day (two are required to reach the Golden Summit) and because of the difficulty of the final stretch, we were told we could go only halfway. "Thank goodness," I muttered to myself, taking all their warnings seriously. We were also told to take our warmest clothes as it would be cold up there. Chinese staff emphasized this many times. Little did they realize how many warm clothes Americans have! So we cheerfully made preparations, but inwardly I was asking questions. Would we have warm enough clothes? (There is snow on the summit.) Would my legs hold out? Would someone fall off a cliff? Would . . . ?

The Starting Point

So here we are at eight o'clock on the drizzly morning of October 2 loading into the bus which would carry us on the first leg of the trek up the mountain. How do you climb a mountain and carry an umbrella at the same time—not to mention that tote bag of extra warm clothing? Feeling quite courageous, fortified with a long night's sleep and an extra iron pill, I had already taken my seat in the bus.

Now here comes Huang Hsin-chyu, our interpreter, with an alternate plan for Mrs. Beechy. Arrangements could be made for me to go in a "sedan car" which would go only part of the way. There would be no English-speaking person in the car, and I would be separated from the group all day, but it would be much more comfortable for me. While he was proposing the sedan car, I had visions of myself regally seated in the old imperial sedan chair, being borne up the precarious trail by six skinny, perspiring coolies.

I finally got the picture straight. Several people from the Tourist Bureau were shepherding a Japanese "guest" from Beijing Institute of Foreign Relations, traveling in a small car with their own driver. The 74-year-old gentleman was not going to attempt the climb. The car could go some places our big bus could not, so he would be able to visit one of the monasteries we would reach on foot. To save the aging American lady from a too rigorous trek, it was suggested that I go with them. They even offered to send along one of our English-speaking staff women, but that would deprive her of the climb.

Huang's question—"What is your opinion?"—put the decision squarely onto my narrow shoulders. Such a big decision on short notice and after I had cranked up my courage for whatever ordeal was presented! First, the negative side of accepting a ride in the sedan car: I would be isolated from the group all day. I would be admitting I was too old and decrepit to climb a few hills. The students would question my ability to handle the China assignment. And I would feel like a loser. At that point I wasn't aware that I'd also miss the opportunity for Buddha's blessing and a long life gained by reaching Longevity Monastery.

On the other hand, if they were that concerned, maybe it was tooth-and-nail, cliff-hanging mountain climbing. Perhaps I'd be even more of a failure by trying and not being able to make it. Perhaps I'd hold up the entire party three-fourths of the way up the hill. Perhaps the mental state of the Chinese entrusted with our care would be jeopardized.

So what if 6,000 Chinese tourists climb it every year? That doesn't mean that an American housewife who spends a lot of time at a desk can. What to do?

At this point some of the students realized what was going on and offered encouragement: "Oh, you can make it, Winnie!" and "We'll carry you if you need a lift." So I boldly declined the sedan car. The die was cast. If I couldn't make it, I'd stay at the monastery. And we were off.

Up We Go Through Damp Mists

At the end of the bus climb we bought sturdy bamboo walking sticks and started up the narrow trail of slippery stepping-stones and slick clay mud, along with numerous Chinese and a few Japanese tourists. Through steeply terraced cornfields and brilliant patches of green leafy vegetables, past rustic hillside homes and blooming wild flowers, past drying herbs and stored rice. We saw the mountain people sawing logs by hand and tending their isolated garden patches. We met the inhabitants padding blithely up and down their familiar walkways. People not only lived up there; people died up there. It was the only place I saw one of the fancy paper-flower wreaths (this one about a yard in diameter) which indicates a death in the household. Since we had to keep a cautious eye on the next step, we stopped occasionally to get a longer view and enjoy the beautiful scenes. The scenery was also an excuse to rest and let our pounding hearts slow down.

Halfway up the mountain trail to the monastery, we came upon a level space big enough for a playground and primary school. Such nice facilities in this remote area? We learned from the principal, no doubt on duty to greet us as it was a holiday, that 200 children come here from the surrounding hills, some walking a distance of eight kilometers morning and evening. That's ten miles a day; no wonder the people are so hardy.

It was not even noon and we'd already reached the monastery grounds. But we could not be too elated. There were still at least 300 cement steps to the top. There a beautifully clean reception room, basins of water for washing, hot tea and fresh pears awaited us. How good these all looked to the mud-spattered, perspiration-soaked Meiguoren (Americans).

White Water Monastery

The master monk, jovial and round in his gray garb with black knitted cap on his shaved head, greeted us and told us a bit of the history of White Water Monastery (commonly called Longevity Monastery because of its promise of long life to persevering climbers), which dates back to 700 AD. The 13 monks now in residence specialize in raising medicinal herbs, treating some patients and even being called for their services at some area hospitals. Besides, they grow beautiful flowers and maintain the grounds and pagodas for the sake of the hordes of visitors. They carefully watch over some treasured relics, including some ancient handwritten Buddhist scriptures. The main attraction is the ancient rotunda, which houses a huge (60-ton) cast-bronze Buddha on an elephant. It is incredible that materials for these were hauled up the mountainside with the transportation facilities of 1,000 years ago.

After a delicious meal in these pleasant surroundings, our energies had been restored for our onward trek. It was downhill now, but that clay is slick and the steps endless. There must have been several thousand stepping-stones (I counted 800 at one point) in the three kilometers to the next monastery. Here we were briefed by the 80-year-old head monk, who looked about 60. He must have made the trip up Longevity Hill and received the Buddha's blessing. We made a short side trip to a lovely waterfall and spectacular gorge. I must confess I sat it out by the waterfall, content with the stately beauty of that spot.

The rest of the way down was relatively easy going, and the sight of that cream-colored Sichuan Teachers' College bus in the village below made the last few kilometers a victory march. The completion of the estimated 14 kilometers was something to celebrate for me and doubtless brought a surge of relief to our Chinese hosts that I had made it under my own steam. (Confidentially, it was not all that bad!)

To round out the "day of the Buddha" we stopped at a pagoda near the entrance to our camp lodgings and attended a worship service from 5:15 to 6:00 p.m. An audience consisting of our group and a few Japanese tourists sat silently while six monks participated in the ritual—chanting, drumming, bowing, kneeling, and making a solemn procession through the audience and around the altar. Compared to the few worshipers inside, there was a large crowd looking in from outside. I suspect this service was reserved for foreign tourists. To the young Chinese with us it was obviously a matter of some interest and curiosity.

Then we went back through the dripping fog of Mount Emei to our third rice meal of the day and an early bedtime for our weary muscles. The next day we would be taking the long drive back "home" to Chengdu. Back to the classes and lectures and field trips and friendships.

Travel by Riverboat

All too soon it was time to pack up for the first leg of our homeward journey and the last fling at seeing the sights of China—five full days from Chongqing (Chungking) to

Shanghai, most of it by riverboat on the mighty Changjiang (Yangtze River). While riverboat travel seems exotic to foreigners, it is the common mode of transportation for thousands of Chinese who live along the shores of China's greatest waterway.

In the early morning darkness at Chongqing, we boarded a small riverboat on which Atlee and I were assigned to a comfortable second-class cabin for two and the students to third-class quarters with eight to a room, all on the second deck. It was only by light of day that we realized the sizable human cargo our little boat was carrying. Passengers were sitting and lying in the corridors even on second deck, while down below they were packed in still more densely. Whenever we stopped at a city or small-town port, many would disembark while a long line of commuters with various sizes and shapes of bundles, baskets, and crates waited to take their places. The river was obviously a major artery for the workaday world; our boat was not just a pleasure launch for vacationers—although we apparently had some of those, too, in our second- and third-class sections of the boat.

A windowed lounge at the front of the boat allowed viewing protected from the raw December wind, but many with their cotton-padded coats braved the weather to get an unhindered view of the passing scene. The rocky coasts on either side formed a gray-brown landscape with a rugged beauty of its own variety. Tiny farms high on hillsides did not look too prosperous, their small cultivated patches carved out of the barren-looking soil. There were stones aplenty for the retaining walls of terraced ridges, which still held the dry remains of a corn crop. Port towns along the way gave evidence of more prosperous, industrial activity. These towns tended to take on the gray-brown hue of the rock and river. But the people on the pier gave evidence of life and gaiety and dynamic energy.

The Three Gorges

The major attraction on the river trip was the fabulous San Xia (Three Gorges), of which we had heard glowing reports. Here the mighty river slices through three mountain ranges which cross its path. The river narrows to 200 or 300 meters with great walls of rock rising to the sky on each side. These almost perpendicular cliffs shut out the rays of the sun except when it is directly overhead. Treacherous rocks have been blasted away to make a safe passage in our day. The first of the gorges we passed through at 5:30 a.m., but some hardy souls were on hand for the tremendous sight. Others of us were content to wait for the daytime navigation of the remaining two, but all agreed that nature's handiwork is indeed awesome.

There are many legends and myths surrounding the famous gorges and the forms and figures which the practiced eye can detect among the mountain peaks. Certain rock formations resemble a stack of books, a sword, a legendary monk with his disciple, and a graceful goddess who watches over one of the gorges. The goddess is one of 12 peaks lining the river. Legends from the third century BC recount how the goddess and her maidens helped the ruler in controlling flood waters, protected inhabitants from wild animals, and guided boatmen through the dangerous waters. Later she and her attendants turned into the 12 peaks and continue to stand guard over the people.

I must say that a first-time viewer finds it difficult to identify these various rocky figures. While we were given literature on the fabled gorges, it was in Chinese, which we, unfortunately, could not read. Folktales also abound showing the heroism of ancient boatmen. They say one can still see the narrow paths cut on the sides of the rocks where men braved the narrow ledges to pull the ropes towing boats upstream against the treacherous current. Today one glides easily through all three gorges within less than a day's time.

The Impossible Dam

In process on the Changjiang River is the Gezhou Dam Project, one of the most complex and ambitious (some say impossible) engineering feats of all times. A giant scheme for water control and hydropower to supply a vast section of the country, it has been called the modern version of the Great Wall. (The dam's first stage was just completed in 1981; the final stage is to be finished by 1985.) Because of this construction we had to leave our boat, be portaged around the project site, and board a second boat. This short overland run gave us a welcome different view of the hill country. There really were people, farms, towns, and cities up there beyond that facade of solid rock. As an added bonus, because there was not enough room in the bus for all, Atlee and I with Mr. Yao got to ride in the jeep which must have been reserved for VIP's. It was the chance of a lifetime—to ride in a jeep with red velvet seat covers!

At Wuhan the river is considerably wider, and we changed boats again to a 1,252-passenger one. Our brief stop did not allow much sight-seeing in this lovely city of wide streets and many trees, which is supposed to be a model for city planning in China. We did drive across the ¾ mile-long, 6-lane bridge over the river. Another engineering triumph, this was the first bridge to be built across the Changjiang. Before its completion in 1958 all north-south transport had to be ferried across the river. A second bridge was built at Nanjing in 1968.

Shanghai and the End of the Tour

The river widened perceptibly as we neared Shanghai with its miles and miles of docks and hundreds of boats of all description. Shanghai has many reminders of the foreign residents of former days; but it is primarily a huge sprawling city, the industrial center of the new China as it was in the old China.

Our memories of Shanghai are perhaps more people oriented than touring centered: A Christmas carol sing with a collection of Westerners at the American consulate on Christmas eve. A midnight mass at the Catholic cathedral with Chinese Christians welcoming the day which commemorates the birth of Christ. An un-Christmasy Christmas day going through airport procedures and saying farewell to our students. A delayed Christmas celebration on the 26th with an American woman (mother of a friend) who left the United States in 1923 to be a missionary in China—she shared with us not only a homey turkey dinner but reminiscences of her life in China as wife of a Chinese doctor and mother of two children in chaotic times of wars and revolutions. An inspiring church service with 2,000 Chinese Protestants the Sunday following Christmas. All good experiences to end our visit.

As we left China, a 30-hour train ride to Guangzhou (Canton) took us through the subtle changes from temperate to tropical climate, where lush greens and bright sunshine signaled us to remove a few layers of our warm clothing. Guangzhou is the Chinese city showing most Western influence, having the most foreign visitors and some interchange with Hong Kong. A short train ride carries the traveler across the border to Hong Kong, that great modern city of skyscrapers, commercial bustle, and shop windows loaded with luxury goods so dear to the hearts of Westerners.

After 4½ months in The People's Republic of China, the glittering display of jewelry, designer garments, and other luxury items was somehow depressing.

Sight-seeing trips eventually come to an end, and we return to the reality of our own everyday world. I hope you have enjoyed the brief glimpses of the new China.

10
Green Bough of Hope

Dreams are often nebulous and fleeting. But the dream for a new China has persisted for most of a century. In the early years the dreamers envisioned a more democratic form of government and release from imperial and feudal tyranny over the powerless masses. Today there remain some 600 members of the Chinese Communist Party and countless other citizens who were active in pursuing that dream in the 1920's. Later the dream was for freedom from colonialism and foreign imperialism.

Memories of the Past

Since 1949, millions of Chinese have shared the hopes for a socialist system which would improve the lives of all the people and build a strong, self-reliant nation. Of the current 38 million party members, who bear major responsibility for the full realization of that goal of prosperity and equality, little more than two million have personal memories of the suffering and sacrifice involved in the achievement of "liberation." In the overwhelmingly youthful population, there is a dwindling proportion of citizens who remember the bitter years of the struggle. But they are not without a dream of their own. So in the 1980's there is some looking back for inspiration and much looking ahead with hope.

The two most influential leaders of the drive to secure those hopes and dreams departed from the scene in 1976, Premier Zhou Enlai on January 8 and Chairman Mao Zedong on September 9. Some others in their 70's and 80's are still at work. Two outstanding women, featured by the Chinese press in 1981, are examples of heroic revolutionary service and unwavering dedication to the cause of an independent China. They have provided role models for more recent generations.

Soong Ching Ling, widow of Dr. Sun Yat-sen, died on May 29, 1981, at the age of 90; her long life had been devoted to improvement of conditions of the common people. She worked along with her husband for the establishment of the Republic in 1911 and continued, after his death in 1925, to give support to the communist cause and the building of the socialist state. This remarkable woman, educated in the United States, was still active in her 80's as head of the China Welfare Institute, devoting herself to women's and children's interests, maintaining international contacts, and writing occasional articles for *China Reconstructs* magazine, which she helped to found 30 years ago. Born in a rich and influential family (sister-in-law to Chiang Kai-shek), she rejected power and wealth for a simple and frugal life-style, which endeared her to all the people. Her political and social contributions were acknowledged by the official bureaucracy, which named her honarary president of the People's Republic. For her the dream lasted a long lifetime in spite of the mistakes and failures which she lived to witness.

Another admired revolutionary figure is Deng Yingchao, widow of Zhou Enlai, who with her husband also dedicated a lifetime, of nearly 80 years, to the building of a new China. From her participation at age 15 in the May 4th Movement of 1919 to the present day as a member of the Political Bureau of the party's Central Committee she has not deviated from her early conviction that the social ideal espoused by the Communist Party was "worth our life's effort and sacrifice" (interview by *China Reconstructs* on the occasion of the 60th anniversary of the CCP). Reading of her early activities—working with the Nationalists in the controversial united front alliance, hounded underground by Chiang Kai-shek's purge, living a hand-to-mouth existence—one would certainly not be surprised if the dream had dimmed. An interesting sidelight: she says that during this period while in hospital for a miscarriage a "dedicated Christian woman doctor" found a safe place for her to recover.

Deng Yingchao accompanied the Long March while in the severe stages of TB, coughing blood as she underwent the rigors of that almost superhuman exploit. (She later made a remarkable recovery during the years at the secluded Yanan headquarters.) After the decades of association with Mao, to whom her very capable husband in a sense played "second fiddle," she remains loyal to the basic rightness of Mao's policies and shows no bitterness at the damage he did to the dream in his declining years. Like Zhou, she is loved and admired by the Chinese masses.

These few examples give us some measure of the tenacity of purpose and long-range perspective of some of the seasoned fighters for freedom from the poverty and oppression endured for centuries in old China. On the other side of the scales we must balance the many thoughtful and questioning members of the younger generation who are tempted to lose faith in the promises for a bright future, who find it difficult to put full trust in their nations' plans and leaders, who become discouraged for lack of immediate, or foreseeable future, improvements. They are left confused by the seesaw

A Chinese student of English with Valerie Gross, her American student/teacher.

of political ideology from right to left and back again. They are sometimes said to be going through a "crisis of belief," and are seeking for something onto which they can pin their hopes.

Deng Xiaoping at the Helm

One character playing a star role in the current drama of Chinese history, Deng Xiaoping, is a good example of that very unpredictability. Deng at age 76 is now chairman of the CCP, leader of one billion Chinese. As early as 1973 he had supported the very policies which are now highly lauded as the Four Modernizations. Although a longtime party official, he was apparently not in accord with the Cultural Revolution and was stripped of all his offices at its outset in 1966. After the most violent stages of the Cultural Revolution subsided, he was reinstated in 1973 as vice premier of the State Council under Zhou—in line of succession to Zhou or Mao. But after the death of Zhou he again came under criticism, especially for his part in an April 1976 disturbance in Tien An Men Square, which appears to have been a spontaneous outpouring of honor and affection for the late premier but was interpreted by Mao and the Gang of Four as a demonstration against their revolutionary line. Deng was again in disfavor.

In the fall of 1976 it was reported that he was involved in investigation of the alleged crimes of the Gang of Four, who were foiled in any plans they may have had for taking power at the death of Mao. In July 1977, Deng Xiaoping was quietly restored to all his former positions, and by 1978 he had again emerged as a national leader. (*Time Magazine* named him Man of the Year for 1978.) In January of 1979 he made history as the first high-ranking PRC leader to visit the United States. By the summer of 1981 he had replaced Hua

Guofeng, Mao's handpicked successor, in the top political office of the land. This resumé of the rise and fall of Deng Xiaoping is an illustration of the uncertainty of the times and a possible explanation of the insecurity leading some young people to take a "wait and see" attitude with regard to the future.

Deng is considered a moderate and a pragmatist. He now has the unenviable task of presiding over the repair of the ravages that the years of intraparty struggle inflicted on the economy and all aspects of society. In 1978 leaders announced plans for a concerted effort to make China a fully modern country by the year 2000, focusing on four areas: agriculture, science and technology, industry, and defense. A three-year period was to be devoted to readjustment and recovery before launching the Four Modernizations program. This adjustment period has now been extended to accord with realism. But the bright hope for the success of modernization has not been abandoned.

We have already noted some of the objectives of this ambitious plan with some conjectures as to the possibility of their achievement. No amateur can predict with any degree of certainty; surprising things sometimes happen in China. We have taken note of various goals as well as the roadblocks to their attainment in many areas of daily life: agricultural production, population control, educational upgrading, health care availability, demand for consumer goods, employment outlook, and economic viability. To North Americans the goal of a $1,000 annual per capita income seems extremely modest, until we remember that present statistics show the average Chinese income to be only about $250 per year. A host of variables could determine the probabilities of success.

On the vital matter of reaching zero population growth in

20 years, there are millions of young couples in the childbearing age-group whose convictions will be a determining factor. As for the desired advancement in science and technology, much depends upon the swift rebounding of higher education as well as the relationships forged with developed countries, the terms on which they are willing to share their expertise and the effectiveness of exchanges which can be negotiated. The great expectations of the Chinese people as a result of China's opening door are tempered by the realism of economic and political limitations. But "hope springs eternal," and there is a sense of optimism and determination.

Evaluation and Reassessment

It is interesting to see what the communist bureaucracy has to say about past efforts to achieve the socialist dream and expectations for future modernization. In July 1981 the CCP celebrated the 60th anniversary of its founding. The world media watched and listened attentively as leaders analyzed and evaluated the past 60 years and passed resolutions which might give clues to the future. Five years after the death of Mao, the new leadership undertook the politically risky task of making a summary statement on the 32 years of the PRC, especially the role of Mao Zedong in that history. The resolution finally agreed upon was of much interest to the Chinese people and to the international community, which has long speculated on the future of China after Mao. As reported by the press, it seems a frank and realistic appraisal of the complex causes of the "ten bitter years" and is to be commended for making no attempt to place all the guilt on the treachery of the Gang of Four.

The resolution emphasizes Mao's great contributions as social theorist, military strategist, revolutionary leader. But it also points out his shortcomings: the mistakes of judgment in his later life; his encouragement of the Mao cult, which tended to isolate him from reality and exaggerate his own importance; and the confusion of right and wrong in his old age, upon which counterrevolutionary cliques (read Gang of Four) were able to capitalize.

The conclusion is that, judging his life as a whole, his contributions far outweighed his errors. His work in founding the CCP, carrying out the war for liberation, establishing the socialist society, building up diplomatic relations and restoring China to her rightful place in international affairs, has earned him a place in the esteem of the Chinese people which can never be forgotten. The resolution admits that chief responsibility for the Cultural Revolution does, indeed, rest with Chairman Mao himself, but the Central Committee and other party leaders must bear some of the blame.

Mao Thought as a guiding philosophy is still to be considered valid although Mao himself violated it in his later years. It is accepted as a synthesis of principles devised by a collective leadership and embodying the Chinese experience of Marxism. Some critics see the care taken to relate the new policies to Mao Thought as an indication that there may still be a sizable body of citizens who would hold more strictly to the old ideology, and question the moderate interpretation now in vogue. This raises the question of whether the new liberalism can continue unchallenged. The success of those liberal policies may be the key to their acceptability.

What Does the Future Hold?

It was made clear that China will continue to develop as a socialist country, striving to correct the mistakes of Mao's last years and to complete the unfinished tasks. But there is to be a stated shift of emphasis from class struggle to economic reconstruction. The 60th-anniversary meeting called for a new revolution—a peaceful revolution in development which promises to be "more arduous than any previous revolution fought with guns, purges and polemics." There was a passing warning that materialism and consumerism must not "overwhelm the life of the spirit committed to socialism." But the basic thrust was for rapid modernization, with a call for well-educated and professionally capable younger leaders, a pragmatic effort to mobilize all resources of the nation in order to recoup the losses and forge ahead.

So it looks as though the Four Modernizations are still the goal. All the people with whom we talked were in agreement with that—the sooner the better! A few had some reservations about the uncertain future. A few raised caution signals with respect to the program's effect on the socialist ideals. We ourselves raise some questions—perhaps

A billboard admonishes, "You'd better have one child only."

more for our own reflection than theirs.

Will the constantly rising expectations of the Chinese exceed the possibilities of their realization in a reasonable amount of time? And will the increased contact with the highly industrialized, affluent West promote impatience with a development plan based on sound principles of self-reliance?

Can our friends in China acquire the positive aspects of modernization (high productivity, improved living standards, luxuries and consumer goods dependent upon exploitation of natural resources, quality education and health care) without incurring the negative aspects (emotional problems, crime, alcohol and drug abuse, sexual irresponsibility, self-centeredness, divorce and family problems, and environmental pollution) which most Western nations are confronting?

Will the Western influences, already apparent in the large cities, dilute the high ideals and service motivations of a socialist society? What will be the psychological impact on youth reared in the context of the group and dependent on social controls when they are exposed to individualism and personal decision-making? (Our group of Goshen College students, of course, experienced the reverse of this problem, which required some adjustment.) Or consider the effect of a traditionally rural society suddenly thrust into the pressures of a highly industrialized situation. Will the strains on the emotional fiber of that society bring a proliferation of psychological problems?

Will the overwhelmingly youthful population without firsthand memory of the old foreign imperialism recognize the dangers of a new imperialism inherent in multinational corporations and powerful interest groups? Will they understand that true development can come only by the primary efforts of those seeking to develop, even though they need the help of outsiders?

I guess my main concern is that in seeking to emulate the West they not become too much like us! I'm confident that thoughtful Chinese are asking some of the same questions. But I'm equally certain that in most cases they would say, "Yes, there are possible injurious side effects, but we are willing to take that risk!" They are prepared for change, and hope is strong within them. To make a play on Mao's metaphor—"The Chinese have stood up"—they are, in fact, off and running.

What Role for Friendship?

The dream of a better life has sustained the Chinese for a long time. Too often in the past 20 years it has been snatched away when it appeared to be materializing. One of the basic ingredients of the Four Modernizations program is the reaching out for friendship and help from developed world neighbors. The highly publicized friendship between the United States and China was a source of some discomfort to us as we prepared to go to China. Was China offering friendship purely for the anticipated science and technology we could supply? Was the United States cultivating the friendship in order to acquire a strategic ally in her longtime feud with the USSR? The huge potential marketplace also attracts some "friendly" notice. Were naive citizens of both great nations being used as political pawns to cement this instant friendship?

As we became acquainted with real, live Chinese and thought of them as our friends, we were all the more opposed to a politically motivated friendship. China is an important nation in her own right; her billion people are a dynamic segment of the world's human resource. As individuals and as bearers of the unique cultural contributions of our respective heritage, we have much to offer and to receive from each other. The fact that we have been cut off from interaction for so many years has allowed the building of myths and stereotypes which only personal contact and informed understanding can erase.

Noted China specialist John S. Service, in his introduction to *The Encyclopedia of China Today* (1979), sheds some light on how these myths were fostered by the policies and attitudes of our own government during the 1940's. He cites the following impediments to understanding: rejection of reality by our government offices, the suppression of unbiased reporting, restricting ourselves to one side in the Chinese struggle, and choosing to analyze available data to conform to our own preconceptions. Negative reporting fostered negative attitudes, which were reinforced by the fear of communism as it became almost an obsession in the 1950's and 60's. Service says that Americans consistently failed to cope with the emergence of China as a world power because our leaders "ignored the facts we knew, . . . cut ourselves off from the facts, . . . looked at the facts through colored glasses and so saw them in distorted form."

China can no longer be ignored. As a peaceful but potentially powerful nation, her policies will have a major impact on the prospects for world peace. China's policies will be partially determined by the responses from the world community to her overtures for relationships and cooperation. The United States' response will be particularly important in the coming years. It is for our own best interests that we Americans become better informed about this large branch of the earth's human family.

While in Chengdu, we were unexpectedly honored by a visit from the U.S. Ambassador, Leonard Woodcock, and his

United States Ambassador Leonard Woodcock and his wife, Sharon (right), with the author at Chengdu in November 1980. Ambassador Woodcock promoted increased Chinese-American understanding.

wife, who joined us for an informal meal ("took potluck" with us, as the interpreter from the Foreign Office put it). Mr. Woodcock's considerable experience with the Chinese had obviously enhanced his appreciation for them. He was impressed with the tremendous changes during his 3½-year tenure and hopeful about future prospects. He felt strongly that China-U.S. relations must be improved for their own sake and not to gain China as a buffer ally against the Soviet Union.

His informed opinion reaffirmed our conviction that Chinese-American friendship should not be prescribed by the political, military, or even economic needs of the moment. To limit it to political opportunism would be a great mistake. The Chinese must be respected in their own right and for their own cultural and historical achievements; friendship must be based on mutual appreciation for the common human aspirations of both sides. Building friendship on the basis of enhanced world understanding rather than as a byproduct of political sloganeering struck us as being more honest and worthwhile. So we opened ourselves to give-and-take with our new friends on grounds of mutual trust and respect rather than expediency or sentimentality.

Open Minds and Hearts

We hope our educational exchange contributed in some small way to the renewal of ties between our two nations, as predicted by the late Premier Zhou Enlai. In a 1956 speech to the National People's Congress, he said, "China proceeds from the desire to co-exist peacefully with all countries, including the United States. . . . Furthermore, we are deeply convinced that the day will come when the Chinese and the American peoples, because of their traditional friendships, will resume their ties through their respective governments."

That day has come. No one knows for how long the two nations will see their future welfare as intertwined, but many Americans have already discovered the Chinese people to be charming, intelligent, and eager participants in many types of exchange. It is a breakthrough for humanity when we can see each other as human siblings rather than proscribed stereotypes, even enemies. One perceptive SST student said she had learned to love, not communism, but communists! I think we all felt something of that sort of liberation from restricting myths.

In a new book by the wife of Edgar Snow (Lois Wheeler Snow, *Edgar Snow's China*), we find a quote from that great interpreter of Mao's revolutionary China, an American journalist considered a true friend to China by all the Chinese with whom we came in contact. This excerpt explains why:

> The truth is that if I have written anything useful about China it has been merely because I listened to what I thought I heard the Chinese saying about themselves. I wrote it down as honestly and as frankly as I could—considering my own belief that it was all in the family—that I belonged to the same family as the Chinese—the human family (P. 269).

I feel this passage exemplifies the open attitude we must take to all people, especially those who differ from us in culture, life-style, or thought patterns. In so doing we make ourselves vulnerable—we may even have to change our preconceived ideas or long-held opinions! But the reward is an enrichment of our own intellectual and cultural lives.

On this note we leave China, with thanks to the many who opened themselves to our friendship and with new appreciation for a proud and capable people.

The Singing Bird

There is an old Chinese saying: "If I keep a green bough in my heart, the singing bird will come." To us it sometimes seems impossible that through the years of pain and bitterness this small bough of hope could be kept from drying up. But the Chinese are a flexible people, who bounce back from disaster with perseverance. During many dark days in the past it must have been difficult to hear the singing bird; but better days did come to vindicate their faith and keep the bough green. Perhaps it is their innate cheerfulness and positive attitude which has kept hope green and ready for the singing bird of happiness and good fortune. As they await a still brighter future, I sincerely hope that singing bird will not delay his return overlong and that our billion friends in the People's Republic of China will always be prepared to welcome him, that they will continue to hear the music in their hearts even when the progress seems slow and the problems insurmountable. They deserve our intelligent understanding, our cooperative goodwill, and our full acceptance as a constructive and creative segment of the human family.

Chronology

Old Stone Age; (Peking man perhaps 400,000)
—500,000-20,000 BC
Legendary Emperor Huangdi; his wife credited with
introducing silk culture—2600-2500 BC
Xia dynasty—2000-1500 BC
Shang dynasty, first fully authenticated dynasty—1500-1000 BC
Zhou dynasty; Great Wall begun in 500—1000-221 BC
Confucius lived from 551 to 479
Qin dynasty; unification of China—221-206 BC
Han dynasty — 206 BC-AD 220
Silk Route opened to central Asia 138 BC
Buddhism introduced from India about AD 170
Six dynasties; sometimes called "dark ages" — AD 220-589
Kingdom of Shu, now Sichuan, 221 to 263
Sui dynasty; excavation of Grand Canal about 604 — 589-618
Tang dynasty — 618-907
Poets Li Bai (701-762) and Du Fu (712-770)
Five dynasties and ten kingdoms under local rulers; no unified
empire — 907-960
Sung dynasty; Genghis Khan united Mongol tribes, captured
Beijing in 1215 — 960-1279
Khubilai Khan ruled Mongol Empire 1251-1294
Yuan dynasty; Mongol rulers (some sources say 1271)
— 1279-1368
Marco Polo served Khubilai Khan 1275 to 1292
Ming dynasty — 1368-1644
Portuguese arrived in China 1514, occupied Macao 1557
Matteo Ricci introduced Western calendar 1610
English arrived in China 1635
Qing dynasty; Manchu rulers — 1644-1911
First American ship arrived in China — 1784
Opium War with British; Treaty of Nanjing, first of
unequal treaties — 1839-42

Taiping Rebellion — 1851-64
Second Opium War with British and French — 1856
Japan defeated China in Sino-Japanese War — 1894-95
China divided into spheres of influence; Open Door Policy — 1899
Boxer Rebellion — 1900-01
Wuchang Uprising under Sun Yat-sen's Nationalists — 1911

Abdication of Yuan emperor; formation of Republic of China — 1912
World War I; China on side of Allies — 1914-18
May 4th Movement protesting terms of Versailles Treaty — 1919
Chinese Communist Party founded in Shanghai — 1921
First United Front of communists and Nationalists to resist Japanese aggression — 1924-27
Chiang Kai-shek's purge of communists — 1927
Chiang's campaigns of extermination against communists — 1931-33
The Long March, communists' retreat to new headquarters in North — 1934-35
Second United Front, encouraged by United States to fight Japan — 1936
Japanese invasion of China — 1937
War of resistance until 1945
World War II; China on side of Allies, Japan defeated — 1941-45
Chinese Civil War between Nationalists and communists — 1946-49
Communists proclaimed Peoples' Republic of China, October 1, 1949
Chiang Kai-shek and Nationalists retreated to Taiwan and established Republic of China there, December 8
Korean War; China aided North Korea and the United States supported South Korea — 1950-53
First Five-Year Plan of PRC — 1953-57
Constitution adopted in 1954
First agricultural communes organized; Great Leap Forward development plan introduced — 1958
Great Proletarian Cultural Revolution, most violent phase from 1966 to 1969 — 1966-76
PRC seated in United Nations, replacing ROC — 1971
American Ping-Pong team invited to Beijing

The New China

President Richard Nixon went to Beijing — 1972
President Gerald Ford visited China — 1975
Deaths of Zhou Enlai and Mao Zedong; Hua Guofeng succeeded Mao — 1976
Gang of Four, including Madam Mao, arrested for Cultural Revolution crimes and plotting to take over government
President Jimmy Carter met with Chinese to work out plans for normalization of U.S.-China relations — 1978
Normalization agreement took effect in January — 1979
Deng Xiaoping visited United States
Deng Xiaoping appointed chairman of Chinese Communist Party — 1981
Zhao Ziyang named premier

Bibliography

Books:

Chiang Yee. *A Chinese Childhood.* New York: W. W. Norton, 1963.

Croll, Elizabeth. *Feminism and Socialism in China.* London, 1978.

Draper, Thomas, ed. *Emerging China.* The Reference Shelf, Vol. 52, No. 1. New York: H. W. Wilson Co., 1980.

Fairbank, John King. *The United States and China.* 4th ed. Cambridge: Harvard Press, 1976.

Frolic, B. Michael. *Mao's People.* Cambridge: Harvard Press, 1980.

Geelan, P. J. M., and D. C. Twitchett, eds. *The Times Atlas of China.* New York: Times Books, 1974.

Haines, J. Harry. *The Twain Shall Meet,* Part III. New York: Board of Global Ministries, The United Methodist Church, 1980.

Kaplan, Frederic M., Julian M. Sobin, and Stephen Andors. *Encyclopedia of China Today.* Updated ed. Fairlawn, N.J.: Eurasian Press, 1980.

Lacy, Creighton. *Coming Home to China.* Philadelphia: The Westminster Press, 1978.

Lawrence, Anthony. *The Love of China.* London: Octopus Books, Limited, 1979.

Leys, Simon. *Chinese Shadows.* New York: Viking Press, 1977.

Lo, Ruth Earnshaw, and Katherine S. Kinderman. *In the Eye of the Typhoon.* New York: Harcourt Brace Jovanovich, 1980.

Lyall, Leslie T. *New Spring in China.* Grand Rapids, Mich.: Zondervan, 1979.

Meyer, Milton W. *China: An Introductory History.* Totowa, N.J.: Littlefield Adams and Co., 1978.

Orr, Robert G. *Religion in China.* New York: Friendship Press, 1980.

Qi Wen. *China: A General Survey.* Beijing: Foreign Language Press, 1979.

Rice, Edward E. *Mao's Way.* Berkeley: University of California Press, 1974.

Ronan, Colin A., and Joseph Needham. *The Shorter Science and Civilization in China* (an abridgment of Joseph Needham's original text), Vol. I. Cambridge, England: University Press, 1978.

Schaller, Michael. *The U.S. Crusade in China, 1938-1945.* New York: Columbia University Press, 1979.

Schell, Orville. *Watch Out for the Foreign Guests!* New York: Pantheon Books, 1980.

Snow, Edgar. *Red Star over China.* New York: Grove Press, 1971 (first published in 1938).

Snow, Lois Wheeler. *Edgar Snow's China.* New York: Random House, 1981.

Ta Kung Pao. *China Handbook.* Hong Kong: Kwong Yi Printing Press, Ltd., 1980.

Tuchman, Barbara W. *Notes from China.* New York: Collier Books, Macmillan, 1972.

_________ *Stilwell and the American Experience in China 1911-45.* New York: Bantam Books, 1971.

Voth, Matilda K. *Clear Shining After Rain.* North Newton, Kan.: Mennonite Press, 1980.

Whitehead, Raymond L. *Love and Struggle in Mao's Thought.* Maryknoll, N.Y.: Orbis Books, 1977.

Whitehead, Raymond L., and Rhea M. Whitehead. *China, Search for Community.* New York: Friendship Press, 1978.

Xue Muqiao. *China's Socialist Economy.* Beijing: Foreign Language Press, 1981.

Yang, C. K. *Religion in Chinese Society.* Berkeley: University of California Press, 1961.

Pamphlet:

CCA Consultation with Church Leaders from China (papers

presented at consultation held in Hong Kong in March 1981). Hong Kong: Christian Conference of Asia, 1981.

Periodicals:

China and the Church Today. Published bimonthly by the Chinese Church Research Center, 7 Kent Road, Flat A, Kowloon, Hong Kong.

China Notes. East Asia/Pacific Office, Division of Overseas Ministries, National Council of Churches, Room 616, 475 Riverside Drive, New York, N.Y. 10115.

China Reconstructs. Published monthly by the China Welfare Institute, Beijing, China.

China Talk. China Liaison Office, World Division, Board of Global Ministries, The United Methodist Church, 2 Man Wan Road, C-17, Kowloon, Hong Kong.

China Update. An occasional newsletter for the China Associates related to the Program Agency of the United Presbyterian Church in the U.S.A., Room 1144, 475 Riverside Drive, New York, N.Y. 10115.

International Bulletin of Missionary Research. Published quarterly by Overseas Ministries Study Center, P.O. Box 2057, Ventnor, N.J. 08406.

The Author

Winifred Nelson Beechy, Goshen, Indiana, a teacher by profession, has maintained an active interest in home and family, service assignments to trouble spots of the world, and peace and reconciliation on the local level as well as worldwide.

Service assignments with Mennonite Central Committee (the relief and development agency for Mennonite and related churches of North America) took her, with her husband Atlee (professor of psychology and peace studies at Goshen College) to post-war Europe, Vietnam, India, Bangladesh, and other Asian and Middle East countries. A school year with the family in India and another year in Indonesia have been valued learning experiences.

The New China is based on the four months which the author and her husband spent in the Peoples' Republic of China as co-directors of a Goshen College student exchange program. Previously the Beechys had accompanied a similar group of Goshen College students on the first Study-Service Trimester in a socialist country—Poland—in 1974.

Winifred holds a BS in education from Goshen College (1938). She earned an MA in peace studies from Associated Mennonite Biblical Seminaries in 1979 and served for several years as coordinator of peace and social concerns for the Mennonite Church. She coauthored two earlier books—*Vietnam: Who Cares?* with Atlee Beechy (1968) and *The Church: The Reconciling Community* with Ray Keim and Atlee Beechy (1970).

Winifred and Atlee are members of College Mennonite Church, Goshen, Indiana, and the parents of three married daughters: Karen Kreider, Judith Dyck, and Susan Enz.